"Dear Unforgettable Brother" THE STAVIG LETTERS

D1518600

Elskede broder Lars Stavik!

Deres meget ærede og længe Venter‑
velse har jeg nu modtaget hvorfor du
takkes derfor og hvoraf jeg Glæder mig
over at se at du endnu ikke har lade(t)
hjerte endnu ikke føle nogen kulde for
‑elige broder som saa ofte tænker paa
‑lienne. Du staar afmalet for mig hver
‑e dag og tanken ogn dig dvæler i mit hje(rte)
‑nhver tid. saa du ikke er uden om mig
‑stund. Jeg ser af det brev at de blev
‑l over mit Potræt og jeg ser at jeg var næs‑
‑endelig for alle andre undtagen du. det
‑ godt thi jeg nu er en Jagtbøse som
‑, saa røk som de er, muligens Beder maa(ske)
dig hvem de Var førend du kjente mig
‑ er at dit brev at du tvivler Saa at du

"Dear Unforgettable Brother"

The Stavig Letters FROM NORWAY

AND AMERICA, 1881–1937

Compiled and annotated by

JANE TORNESS RASMUSSEN

and JOHN S. RASMUSSEN

with essays by EDVARD HOEM

and BETTY A. BERGLAND

SOUTH DAKOTA

STATE HISTORICAL SOCIETY PRESS

Pierre

This publication is funded, in part, by the
GREAT PLAINS EDUCATION FOUNDATION, INC.,
Aberdeen, S.Dak.

Library of Congress Cataloging-in-Publication data
Stavig, Lars A., 1844–1933.
"Dear unforgettable brother": the Stavig letters from Norway and America,
1881–1937 / compiled and annotated by Jane Torness Rasmussen and John S.
Rasmussen; with essays by Edvard Hoem and Betty A. Bergland.
    pages cm
Includes index.
ISBN 978-0-9860355-6-2 (alk. paper)
1. Stavig, Lars A., 1844-1933—Correspondence. 2. Norwegian Americans—
South Dakota—Day County—Correspondence. 3. Norwegian Americans—
South Dakota—Day County—Social life and customs. 4. Immigrants—South
Dakota—Day County—Correspondence. 5. Immigrants—South Dakota—
Day County—Social life and customs. 6. Day County (S.D.)—Social life and
customs. 7. Stavig, Knudt—Correspondence. 8. Norwegians—Correspondence.
I. Stavig, Knudt. II. Rasmussen, Jane Torness. III. Rasmussen, John S.
IV. Title. V. Title: Stavig letters from Norway and America, 1881–1937.
F657.D3S73 2013
978.3´14203—dc23   2013026628

Printed in the United States of America

The paper in this book meets the guidelines for permanence and durability
of the committee on Production Guidelines for Book Longevity of the Council
on Library Resources.

Text and cover design by Rich Hendel

Please visit our website at www.sdshspress.com

17 16 15   2 3 4 5

Dedicated to Harold L. Torness,
whose love for family, place, and stories
brought this project to life

Contents

INTRODUCTION

The Saga of the Stavig Letters

JANE TORNESS RASMUSSEN

On the rugged west coast of Norway where the Romsdal peninsula juts out into the Norwegian Sea, the farm called Knutgarden sits on a small rise of ground overlooking the fjord. The house and barn lie in the shadow of an enormous rock known as Storhaugen, "the great rock." Along this barren stretch of land between the ocean and the mountains, generations of Staviks have fished the rough seas and farmed the rocky ground. This place was the home Lars Stavig had left in 1876, the place he would hold in memory when he wrote his letters back to Norway over the next fifty years. From here, his half-brother Knut Stavig would send news of the family and friends Lars would never see again. Neither man could have known that their collected correspondence would one day bring the immigrant experience to life for those who had never lived with a divided heart.

The Knutgarden farmhouse became home to other generations, including that of Kåre Stavik, who grew up there during the 1930s. In the house were two cabinets he and his ten siblings were not allowed to open or touch, he recalls. One cabinet, which was kept locked in the basement, contained ammunition for the family's firearms. The second was the corner cupboard in the living room that held the treasured "America letters" written by Lars to Knut, Kåre's grandfather. Over five decades, the two men—and other members of their families—exchanged more than two hundred letters, all handwritten in Norwegian. These brothers, fishermen and farmers with little formal education, would not have been accustomed to letter writing. What motivated them to keep up this correspondence, and why were the letters so important to them?

The Knutgarden farmhouse that Lars Stavig and his family left in 1876 stands next to Storhaugen, "the great rock," in Stavik, Norway. (Stavig House Museum, Sisseton, S.Dak.)

A complicated family history makes the bond between the two brothers especially significant. Lars Stavig, born in 1844, was the only child of Andreas and Marit Stavig, but he was not an "only" child. Marit was a widow with five sons when Andreas married her. When Lars was a year and a half old, she and her two eldest sons died of typhoid fever. Left alone with four young children, Andreas Stavig married Brit Knutsdotter Haukas, and the couple had five more children, including Knut Stavig, born in 1851. The older children and the younger children were not related, but Lars was a half-brother to them all.

Andreas died when Lars was sixteen years old, and his step-mother Brit married a man named Knut Ellingson and bore more children to whom Lars was not related. As the oldest son of his father, Lars inherited Knutgarden with the provision that he pay one-fifth of its value to each of his five younger half-brothers and sisters. In addition, according to the custom in Norway at the time, older relatives who lived on a family farm were entitled to *kaar*, a lifelong income from the property. The stepmother and her husband, who were still young and had lived on the farm only a short time, demanded this entitlement. Within a few years, Lars had his own wife and family and objected to supporting these able-bodied persons for the rest of their lives. He began to consider seeking his fortune in America.

Although Lars owned rather than rented his land, life was not easy. Cultivation was laborious, the growing season was short, and crop failures were common. Like generations before him, Lars braved the dangers of fishing during the winter months. "It is not very pleasant to go out thirty or forty miles in a small open boat in the middle of winter in this cold northern climate," he wrote in his memoir. "Very often a husband and father was never heard from again when he went out on one of these fishing trips."[1]

Such difficult conditions—combined with concerns for the future of their sons Andrew, Hans, and Magnus—led Lars and his wife, Maren Hustad, to decide to leave. In May of 1876, the family packed their possessions and walked down to the water. They boarded a rowboat manned by Maren's younger brother, who took them the forty kilometers (just over twenty-four miles) down the

Romsdal Fjord to the port city of Molde. From there, the family rode a small coastal steamer to the seaport of Bergen. A small ship took them from Bergen to Germany, where they embarked on a larger ship headed for America. Relatives in Norway said that when four-year-old Hans boarded the rowboat leaving Stavik, he turned to his father and said that he would never see Norway again.[2] The family arrived in the United States and in June 1876, they reached Morris, Minnesota.

My grandmother, Anna Stavig, was three years old in 1884 when her parents Lars and Maren, now with five children, left Minnesota in a covered wagon pulled by a team of oxen and traveled one hundred miles to a homestead in Dakota Territory. Anna was a young woman living at home in 1901 when nineteen-year-old Ole Torness, newly arrived in Webster, South Dakota, learned there was a family nearby from the same area he had recently left in Norway. He walked twenty-four miles one Sunday to meet them. Ole and Anna were married in 1904 and raised a family of ten children in Sisseton, including my father, Harold Torness. Ole, who had been orphaned at age five, eventually earned enough money to bring his four siblings to South Dakota.

In 1967, my father took our family to Norway, a trip that left a deep impression upon me as a seventeen-year-old. I knew the journey was no typical family vacation when, upon reaching Romsdal, my father knelt to kiss the ground. It had been his dream to take his family to the homeland of his grandparents and his father. It was a revelation to me to visit the communities of Tornes, Stavik, Holm, Vevang, Hustad, and Gule, names I recognized as belonging to the older generation who gathered around our dining-room table at family gatherings. The names that were places on a map in Norway had been adopted as family names by those who emigrated.

At the settlement of Stavik, we visited Knutgarden, where Lars grew up and where his half-brother Knut married Anna Bendiksdatter, raised his family of five children, and lived until his death in 1950 at the age of ninety-nine. We were guests of Knut's only son, Andreas, who had taken over the farm from his father in 1924. In the living room of the farmhouse, Andreas unlocked the corner cupboard and introduced Harold to the America letters. As their caretaker since his father's death, Andreas barely allowed Harold to handle the prized letters, much less read them. Harold was captivated by the discovery, however, knowing that each letter, folded in its original envelope, could tell the story of how South Dakota had become home to our family.

Born in 1919, Harold had spent his formative years in the company of his Grandpa Lars in Sisseton. Lars had never learned English, so the grandchildren knew him only as well as they knew the Norwegian language, and for Harold, that was fairly well. Still, as a young boy, he was more interested in the bag of candy that Grandpa Lars always brought when he visited the Torness house than in listening to Lars converse in Norwegian with Anna as she worked in the kitchen. Once he saw the letters that spanned five decades, however, Harold realized he had another opportunity to know his grandfather through their contents. What might he learn about Lars's decision to leave Norway, his early years in Minnesota, homesteading in Dakota Territory, and raising his children there? So many stories had been lost when Anna died suddenly in 1931, leaving twelve-year-old Harold and his eight siblings behind, but in Norway, Andreas was the keeper of the keys—and the answers to Harold's questions would remain locked with the letters in the corner cupboard.

The 1967 trip gave Harold an even deeper connection to his Romsdal roots. Of our time in Norway, my father wrote back to his sisters and brothers in the Midwest, "Everyone came to the ferry. . . . They waved to us until we were out of sight. . . . We now know about that place where all our Stavig and Torness ancestors came from and we will never forget the ground, mountains, rocks, water, and its wonderful people."[3]

The summer of 1976 marked the centennial of Lars and Maren's emigration from Norway, a milestone that required special commemoration. With Harold at the helm, 125 Stavig descendants, including descendants of Knut Stavig from Norway, met at Inherred Lutheran Church near Starbuck, Minnesota, in June. It had been one hundred years since Lars and Maren first worshiped at the church upon arriving to start their new life in America. The anniversary message was given by Lawrence Stavig, the eldest grandson

(Opposite)
This 1882 map of Romsdal in western Norway shows the port city of Molde (bottom center) and the fishing village of Bud (upper left), both significant locations in the correspondence of Lars and Knut Stavig. Scattered across the map are place names that many of those who emigrated adopted as surnames upon arriving in America. (Stavig House Museum, Sisseton, S.Dak.)

of Lars and Maren and the long-time president of Augustana College in Sioux Falls, South Dakota. He recounted family stories of the couple's concerns about leaving their religious traditions behind and their overwhelming joy at finding a new congregation organized by people of their own nationality.

Lawrence Stavig was the link between generations of Stavigs in Norway and America. Lawrence and his father, Magnus, were the first of Lars's descendants to return to Norway. In 1937, Lawrence, then a Lutheran pastor in Northfield, Minnesota, attended a worldwide church conference in England. Magnus accompanied him, and father and son took the opportunity to travel to Romsdal, where they stayed with Knut on the family farm, or, as Magnus had referred to it, "the place where my cradle once stood."[4] The story is told by relatives in Norway that the blanket under which Lawrence and Magnus slept during their visit was later cut in half so that relatives could share the keepsake with their families.

Lawrence wrote to Knut later that year: "You will never know how much happiness the opportunity to come to Norway and especially to [Stavik] gave us. . . . We often marveled over your strength and power, that you could travel with us day and night—and you a man of over eighty years. . . . When I left Bergen, over the ocean to England, it was almost as if I was leaving my home. I looked back toward Bergen's mountains—Norway's coast—and felt the tears come to my eyes."[5]

The letters from Magnus and Lawrence to Knut following their time in Norway complete the set of America letters that Andreas carefully looked after at Knutgarden. When Andreas died in 1980, Kåre, the second-oldest son in the family, told his mother, Betsy, that he wished for nothing but to inherit the America letters. Kåre Stavig and Harold Torness had met at a family wedding in Norway in 1976, at which time Kåre first learned of Harold's interest in Lars's letters. As the owner of an electronics store in Molde, Kåre could respond to Harold's request for copies of the correspondences. Copy machines, which were unknown to Andreas's generation, made it possible for the grandson of Knut to provide the grandson of Lars with duplicates of the America letters.

In a letter to Harold in 1984, Kåre wrote, "These old letters you talk about are now on the way to [the] USA. A daughter of my wife's cousin has been here in Molde since July. She travelled to San Francisco last Sunday. She will send the letters to you when she comes home. I hope they will reach you in good condition, and you will get a terrible work to read them. I think you will have enough hobby for this winter."[6]

Harold now had hundreds of pages of his grandfather's letters written in his own hand, from the strong cursive of the early years to the wobbly ciphers of old age, and it did not take him long to discover that his childhood exposure to the Norwegian language had not prepared him for the task of translating written text. When Harold's cousin Evelyn Boyer introduced him to her friends Marta and Bruce Boyce in Minneapolis, the problem of finding a capable translator was solved. A native of the west coast of Norway, Marta Boyce was fluent in both Norwegian and English, and she was familiar with the dialect used in the letters. Once the box containing Lars's correspondence arrived, however, she was overwhelmed by the magnitude of the collection. The translation process became a team effort with her husband, Bruce, who had studied Norwegian at Luther College in Decorah, Iowa. Together, they spent countless hours outside of their regular jobs translating the letters.

During the nearly two decades between first seeing Lars's letters in Norway and finally getting copies of them, Harold Torness wondered what had happened to Knut's letters to Lars. If the America letters were so valuable to the family in Norway, there must be a parallel story for the letters that had come to America. The search would present a different set of challenges than had the locked corner cupboard at Knutgarden. After spending eight years in Pope County, Minnesota, Lars and Maren and their five children had packed their belongings and set out for their homestead in Nutley Township, Dakota Territory. There they spent twenty-five busy years developing the homestead and raising seven children (two more were born in South Dakota). When Maren died in 1908, Lars rented out his land and moved into an upstairs room in the home of his son Peter in nearby Sisseton. Could Knut's letters to Lars have been lost during one of those moves?

After Maren's death, Lars lived on for another twenty-five years, and his letters to Knut became more poignant. Lars confided in his brother about the loneliness of losing his wife and the pain of leaving his beloved homestead. The growing use of the English language by his family and church alienated Lars from everyday life. Writing to his brother in his native language kept him connected to his past and his memories of Norway. Lars was eighty-eight years old when he wrote his last letter to Knut in December 1932, just seven months before he died.

Fifty years after Lars's death, Harold Torness led the search for Knut's letters among the generations of Stavig descendants. Certain that Lars would have treasured the letters just as Knut had, Harold made telephone calls and wrote to relatives, encouraging them to look for the correspondence. He and his cousin Mathilda Stavig, both walking with canes, explored the contents of the three floors of the Andrew Stavig home in Sisseton where Mathilda had spent her life, thinking that the family home of Lars's eldest son would be a likely location, but nothing surfaced. The search finally met with success in 1994 when Harold received a telephone call from Dorothy Stavig in Sacramento, California, announcing that she had found Knut's letters to Lars in the bottom of a trunk in her garage.

A metal box held the collection, each letter in the envelope in which it had been mailed. Dorothy's husband Alf, another of Harold's cousins, had passed away in January 1993, and she had spent more than a year going through his personal belongings. For years, Alf and Harold had maintained a lively correspondence about a variety of topics, including family history and their trips to Norway. Alf had uncovered many historical and family documents that he shared with Harold, but neither of them realized that Alf's father Edwin, the youngest child of Lars and Maren, had been the keeper of Knut's letters. After Edwin and his wife Lydia died, Alf and Dorothy inherited the trunk. It stood in the back of their garage for years, but they never thoroughly explored the contents.

Dorothy had a passion for family history and a skill for organizing. In the midst of settling her husband's estate, she took time to inventory the letters and make copies for Marta and Bruce Boyce for phase two of the translation process. The Boyces were eager to discover the "other side" of the story. Once the translation was complete, Harold Torness had copies of the English versions of the letters printed in two volumes for relatives. He then donated copies of the complete set of letters in Norwegian and the two volumes of translated letters to the Center for Western Studies at Augustana College in Sioux Falls. Harold also kept a copy in the back office of the Roberts County National Bank in Sisseton, where he juggled banking, writing stories for the local newspaper, and conversing over coffee.

In January 1996, Wayne Knutson and his wife Esther of Vermillion, long-time family friends from the Sisseton area, stopped to visit Harold. As he showed them the volumes of the letters, he related his emotional response to them and asked Knutson, professor emeritus of the theater department at the University of South Dakota, whether he thought the essential story of the two brothers could be extracted and brought to life. A lively discussion ensued, and by the time the last drop of coffee disappeared, Knutson had agreed to develop a theatrical piece based on the correspondence.

Wayne Knutson spent his winter vacation in Texas immersed in the letters, about which he wrote: "I have spent many hours reading and rereading all of the translated, available letters exchanged between Lars and Knut Stavig and their relatives. I think they are invaluable in reflecting the immigrant experience in America, as well as the 'mind set' of those who stayed in the Old Country. The letters delineate the differences between those who caught the American fever and came over and those who decided to 'stay put.' Though the letters were written by Norwegians, they have enough human universality to reflect the nineteenth century immigrant experience of those from any country."[7]

In another progress report, Knutson stated: "I have become convinced that the treatment should take the form of a readers' theatre vehicle. . . . One of the readers would serve as a narrator to offer fact, transition, and continuity; the other two readers would read selected excerpts directly from the letters. Though only a small number of the total words will be used, there will be enough to dramatize the immigrants' dreams, ambitions, family joys and griefs, and cultural progress (both intimately and universally), while also making a commentary upon the times and the

Stavik den 4de Februar 1887,

Elskede broder Lars Stavik!

Deres meget ærede og længe Ventede
skrivelse har jeg nu modtaget hvorfor du hjer-
telig takkes derfor og hvoraf jeg Glæder mig meget over at se at du endnu ikke har ladet
dit hjerte endnu ikke føle nogen kulde for din
kjødelige broder som saa ofte tenker paa dig
og dienne. Du staar afmalet for mig hver.
eneste dag og tanken ogn dig dveler i mit hjerte
til enhver tid. saa du ikke er uden om mig nogen stund. Jeg ser af det brev at de blev meget
Glad over mit Potrat og jeg ser at jeg var nesten
ukjendelig for alle andre untagen du. det gjor-
de jeg godt thi jeg nu er en Gagebuse som man
siger, saa røk som de er, muligens Peder maatte
sige dig hvem de Var forend du kjente mig igjen.
Jeg ser af dit brev at du tvivler paa at du ikke
faar se mit kjødelige ansigt forend at du
kommer tilbage til os. det havde været Gladelig
for os at du kom saa langt engang

American dream. Concurrently, we would communicate the counterpoint from the Norwegian perspective, as written by those who decided to stay put."[8]

In the same month that Knutson met with Harold Torness, the Heritage Museum of Roberts County gained possession of the ten-bedroom Victorian home built by Andrew and Mary Stavig for their family in 1916. Andrew's daughter Mathilda bequeathed the house, which had remained in the family for eighty years and was still in its original condition, to the museum in her will. What venue could be more appropriate for a performance of the letters than the family home of Lars's eldest son? With Knutson's approval, planning began for the premiere of *The Stavig Letters: The Story of a Norwegian Immigrant* in the parlors of the Stavig House Museum. More than two hundred fifty people from eight states and Norway attended a weekend conference that marked the official opening of the Stavig House Museum in the fall of 1996. In addition to three public performances of the readers' theater, scholars offered presentations on the architecture of the home and the larger story of Scandinavian immigration.

The Stavig house came to life on a warm Friday night in October 1996 when seventy descendants of Lars and Maren gathered for a special premiere of the readers' theater. One hundred twenty years had passed since Lars and Knut had parted, never to see each other again. That night, the private letters that had kept their brotherly bond alive would be read publicly for the first time. Knut's grandson, Kåre Stavik, travelled from Norway to honor that bond with Lars's grandson, Harold Torness. The audience included Dorothy Stavig and her daughters, along with translators Marta and Bruce Boyce—the people without whom the letters would not have come together.

Knutson selected and directed the cast of three for the first performance: Art Johnson, a classmate from Sisseton, in the part of Lars; John Rasmussen, my husband, in the part of Knut; and our daughter Sarah Rasmussen, great-great-granddaughter of Lars Stavig, as the narrator. Veteran theater director though he was, Knutson admitted to being nervous about that initial reading before so many family members. His fears were unfounded. The voices of the two brothers broke through the decades of separation and the ocean between them, and the family entered the powerful immediacy of their letters, composed in the moment, with no knowledge of what the future held. Woven through the letters were the dreams and aspirations, the joys and griefs of the two brothers—one who came to the prairie and one who stayed by the sea.

Just as the personal connection of the story resonated with family, the response from those attending the public performances that weekend presaged broader interest in *The Stavig Letters* readers' theater. Audience members not only reflected on their own family stories of immigration but also responded to the letters' authentic first-person perspective on world events. Lars's letters cover the arrival of the railroads on the prairie, changes in agriculture, the advent of aviation, World War I, the influenza pandemic of 1918–1919, and the Great Depression. Knut's letters tell not only of personal struggles but also of the state of the Norwegian economy, the dangers of traditional fishing practices, and changes in Norwegian religion and culture.

Knutson's contribution to the project cannot be overstated, and this volume reflects his efforts. His connection to Sisseton, his lifetime of work in the theater, and his passion for the project were the perfect fit for the challenge of editing nearly two hundred pages of single-spaced type into a seventy-minute reading. He established strict rules for himself about following the chronology of the letters, keeping the original wording, using portions of nearly all of the brothers' letters, and adding narrative only when necessary. Within these boundaries, he also sought to balance pathos with humor while remaining true to the integrity of each brother's character as expressed in the letters. As a scholar, Knutson was motivated by his own curiosity. "I have always been intrigued with the decision of some to come to America and some who decided to stay in the old country," he wrote. "*The Stavig Letters* provide a marvelous testimony of those who came and of those who stayed put."9

Since that first performance in 1996, the readers' theater has been presented more than sixty times in a four-state area and in Scandinavia. Common threads emerge from every audience during the discussions that follow the readings. Regardless of the country their families came from, audience members connect to the universal themes of leaving home, adjusting to a new place, desiring a better life for one's children, living with the difficulties of aging, and struggling to balance the old and the new.

Rasmus Sunde, a Norwegian historian and writer, attended a performance of *The Stavig Letters* at Augustana College while serving as a guest professor there in 2005. He recognized the uniqueness of the collection from a Norwegian perspective. Sunde was aware of many letters in Norway that had come from America but had never encountered such an extensive collection of family correspondence from both sides of the ocean. As a historian, he was interested in how the letters, spanning half a century, document change in the two societies. He contacted the Romsdal Historical Association and proposed a book that would make the collection known in Norway. Sunde researched the letters at the Center for Western Studies and worked with the Stavig House Museum to obtain photographs and interpretation. In Norway, he consulted with Kåre Stavik and the Romsdal Museum in Molde. Sunde's book, *Amerikabrev 1880–1950: Livssoga til to brør frå Romsdal*, published in 2009, has been well received in Norway.

That same year, James P. Sprecher, executive producer at South Dakota Public Broadcasting, attended a performance in Vermillion specifically to hear Knutson, his former professor, read the part of Lars Stavig. Sprecher envisioned a television documentary based on the letters and set out to pursue the possibility. A media grant from the South Dakota Humanities Council helped to fund the project, which included filming on the prairie where Lars homesteaded and in Romsdal, Norway. The Stavig House Museum provided readers, actors, family history, photographs, and a filming venue in the historic home. The documentary premiered in Sisseton in February 2011 and has aired on public television stations nationwide. It received a Regional Emmy for Historical Documentary from the Upper Midwest Chapter of the National Academy of Television Arts & Sciences in September 2011. The following year, *The Stavig Letters* received the History Content Award from the National Educational Telecommunications Association.

The original letters of Lars and Knut provided the basis for the readers' theater, the book in Norway, the television documentary, and now this book, each contributing to the understanding of the immigrant experience. As these projects were being developed, the original letters remained in the homes of the third generation "keepers"—Kåre Stavik in Molde, Norway, and Dorothy Stavig in Sacramento, California.

On one of Dorothy's trips to Norway, Kåre invited her to visit the archives of the Romsdal Museum in Molde. Kåre had decided it was time to find a permanent home for the America letters he had inherited, and he recommended depositing them in the Romsdal Museum archives. After their visit, Dorothy agreed to discuss the disposition of Knut's letters with family members in the United States. Eventually, Lars's descendants decided that the letters of the two brothers should be held as one collection in their native country, where scholars could study them in the dialect in which they were written.

Kåre Stavik donated his set of America letters to the Romsdal Museum in 2009. In the spring of 2010, my husband John and I traveled to Sacramento to pick up the original letters of Knut Stavik from Dorothy Stavig and hand-carry them back to South Dakota. In Pierre, the staff of the State Archives program of the South Dakota State Historical Society produced electronic copies, scanning each original letter and accompanying envelope in order to complete the set of letters available to researchers in Lars's adopted state.

Then, in July 2010, we had the privilege of returning Knut's letters to Norway. In a simple ceremony attended by Knut's grandson Kåre Stavik and his wife Oddbjorg, we presented the letters to the curator and staff of the Romsdal Museum in Molde as reporters covered the event. That evening, we gathered with Stavik relatives in the living room of the old farm home at Knutgarden to watch the news story on national television about the reuniting of the two brothers' letters. In the lingering summer light, we sat on the front porch eating strawberries and fishcakes in the shadow of Storhaugen, the great rock that looks to the sea.

NOTE ON THE EDITING

The letters presented here are transcribed from the translations of the original correspondence of Lars and Knut Stavig and represent an expanded version of those selected for *The Stavig Letters* readers' theater. In a few instances, information has been inserted in brackets to clarify the identities of people or places. Omitted passages, often news about family acquaintances that will not hold meaning for today's readers, are noted with ellipses. Short narrative passages have also been inserted where needed to explain events or cover the passage of time; they appear in italics. Finally, notes have been added to supply more detailed information.

Although the letters appear in chronological order, they do not necessarily alternate between the brothers. From the period between March 1887 and March 1896, for example, any letters Knut may have written to Lars appear to have been lost; therefore, he is heard from here only once before 1896. Likewise, the brothers sometimes went months or years without corresponding.

While the Stavig Letters collection is composed largely of Lars's and Knut's correspondence, it contains correspondence from other relatives, as well. Included here are occasional letters from Lars's daughter Louise and sons Magnus, Andrew, and Hans, grandson Lawrence, and Lars's stepsister Sirianna Aas and niece Anna Svino in Norway.

The spellings of proper names also vary. The brothers, especially Knut, typically used the old Norwegian spellings of "Knudt" and "Stavik." Many names have changed in Norway since the late 1800s. Before that time, Norway and Denmark had a common written language that was based on Danish. Around 1900, Norwegians began to work toward a written language that would be closer to spoken Norwegian. The result was two written languages: Nynorsk ("New Norwegian"), which is based on Norwegian dialects, and Bokmål (literally translated as "book tongue"), more similar to Danish. In addition, many immigrants began to use anglicized versions of their given names as time passed. Readers will therefore see Lars's sons Andreas, Peder, and Edvin also referred to as Andrew, Peter, and Edwin.

NOTES

1. Lars A. Stavig, *Memories* ([Sisseton, S.Dak.]: By the Author, n.d.), p. 6.

2. Harold Torness to family, 29 Aug. 1967, author's collection.

3. Ibid.

4. Magnus Stavig to Knut Stavig, 3 May 1905, Stavig Letters, acc. no. H2010-052, State Archives Collection, South Dakota State Historical Society, Pierre.

5. Lawrence Stavig to Knut Stavig, 10 Dec. 1937, ibid.

6. Kåre Stavig to Harold Torness, Christmas 1984, author's collection.

7. Wayne Knutson to Michael F. Haug, 20 June 1996, ibid.

8. Memorandum, Wayne S. Knutson to Stavig House Committee, 9 Apr. 1996, author's collection.

9. Quoted in *Sisseton Courier*, 25 Sept. 1996.

The Stavig Letters

Annotated by JOHN S. RASMUSSEN

Lars and Maren Stavig and their three boys left Norway for the United States from the port city of Molde, shown here in 1890. (Romsdalsmuseet, Molde, Norway)

In May of 1876, thirty-two-year-old Lars Stavig, his wife, Maren Hustad Stavig, and sons, Andrew, age seven, Hans, age four, and Magnus, age two, left Romsdal, Norway,[1] seeking a brighter future in the United States. Lars left behind three half-brothers, two half-sisters, and his stepmother. It was Knut, the second oldest, to whom Lars felt the closest and with whom he would correspond for the next fifty years. Lars and his family arrived in Morris, Minnesota, in June of 1876 and went to live and work with Einar Johnson, a bachelor who farmed near White Bear Center. Three years later, the family moved to the railroad land nearby, where they became "squatters," which meant that they would have first chance to buy the land from the railroad, when and if it was put on the market.

White Bear Centre [Minn.]

January 24, 1881

Dear unforgettable brother, Knut A. Stavig,

. . . . America is good for everyone and especially for people that have small farms in Norway and then come here. We have not left much behind that we feel sorry about. . . .

Dear brother, if you believe what I'm writing, you know my true feeling about America. In all sincerity, if you would like to come, it is best to come before you have anything in Norway you desire. You can visit me next summer, and if you don't like it, you can make enough money next summer to travel back and forth as you like. . . .

Don't let the Devil rule over you. Find yourself a woman, K. A. Stavig. . . .

Lars A. Stavig

White Bear Center

November 21, 1881

I'm 36 years old the 21st of November

Dear Brother Knudt Stavig,

. . . I want to tell you that there is a lot of work to be had here. They are building two railroad tracks, 2 to 3 miles between. The closest to my home is only 1½ miles away. Only three miles away, they are laying out a plan for a new town.[2] That is where we will deliver our wheat next fall. The railroad work is over for the fall, but in the spring the work will start again in earnest. The pay for a grown man is $2 a day, and it is $4 if he has a horse. . . .

I won't mince words but will come right out and tell you how I feel. Dear brother, I don't feel it is right for you to stay at home any longer and waste your time working on sea and land and only receive shame and bad words as thank you. I feel it would be better for you to come to America. . . .

I hear, dear brother, that you think it is not going well for me. I must answer you about that. I have none of the world's riches which can be counted in so many thousand dollars in money. I have my

Maren and coffee for my house the whole year. I live in my *kvite-brødsdager* ["white bread days"]. . . .

But if you want to stay home, don't let me tear you away. If you don't try anything, you will never know how it will work out. You must try it to find out.

From Lars Stavig

After squatting on the railroad property for several years and having no money to buy the land they were living on even if it were to come up for sale,[3] Lars decided to take a homestead claim in Dakota Territory. In the fall of 1883, he filed on two quarters of land in Day County. The following year, the Stavigs and three other families left Starbuck, Minnesota, and traveled one hundred miles by oxen and covered wagon to Roslyn, Dakota Territory. The trip took eight days.[4] After leaving Browns Valley, Minnesota, and entering Dakota Territory, they began to cross the Sisseton-Wahpeton Indian Reservation and ascend the Couteau des Prairies, or Prairie Coteau, a high plateau that extends throughout eastern South Dakota. It was then that Lars felt the loneliness of the wilderness, a wide expanse of prairie without a house in sight. The family settled in Nutley Township in Day County, a few miles north of the newly established town of Webster, where they would live for the next twenty-five years.

Knut Stavig was nearing thirty years of age when he posed for this photograph, taken in Norway in 1880. (Stavig House Museum, Sisseton, S.Dak.)

Stavik [Norway], February 4, 1887

Beloved Brother Lars Stavik

I have now received your much-honored and long-expected writing, for which you are heartily thanked. I am very happy to see that you still have not let your heart feel any coldness toward your brother in the flesh, who so often thinks about you and yours. . . .

Now I must tell a little about myself. First, I must tell you that this winter I shall row for fish together with Hans E. Karlsnas. It is now four years since I rowed for any fish. I must complain that I am not looking forward to this task, as you know. But if God preserves me this time, then, it shall be the last time I go rowing.[5] . . .

I was very surprised at the large animal which you have. There is certainly many kilograms of usable meat on such an oxen and much milk and butter that you get, also. . . . That you have more than enough, I can understand. But what use is the milk that you get from so many cows? . . .

Stavik's fishing group had a large catch at Lilleviksneset, so they got 280 crowns per person and a little extra for the net. I have six nets, and from them I earned 50–60 crowns, and that was very good. . . .

I must tell you that here . . . there are many people that are leaving for America this spring, especially, young people and boys.

From your brother K. Stavik

Nutley

March 11, 1887

Unforgettable Dear Brother,

Knudt A. Stavig

. . . Our largest, closest town, Webster, is about two Norwegian miles from our home.[6] The town is about six years old so it is understandable that this newly settled area is not well to do yet. You can't think or expect that a man with a large family who had to borrow the money for tickets to come here should be able to repay it the first fall. It will take the first year to fulfill the minimal needs of the family.

We are not gathering gold off from the streets. It is easy to earn

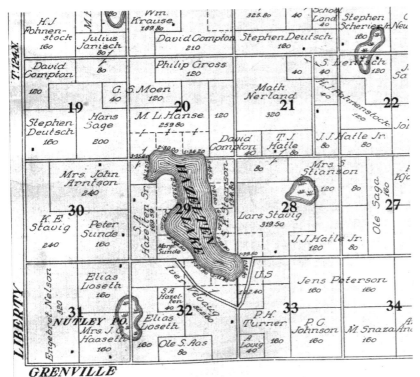

This detail of the southwest corner of Nutley Township shows the homestead of Lars Stavig situated in Section 28. (South Dakota State Historical Society, Pierre)

money, and it is easy to spend it. A willing and hard working man can improve himself year by year and eventually become an independent owner of much land.

You asked how much milk we got from a cow. Most cows give a medium bucket of milk. A very good cow will give more. You ask what we use the milk for. We give it to the calves and the pigs. If you have 12 cows, you also have 12 calves. They will take all the milk they can get. You ask how much butter we get. It can be different each time. . . . The butter we have left, we take to town and exchange for coffee and sugar and other things that we need. The butter is cheap. We would get from 6 cents to 18 cents a pound. . . .

Here is a happiness, dear brother, that is beautiful. There is nothing here that I'm afraid to write about. Everything I tell you is true. I would think you knew me well enough to know that I would not lie to you. . . .

I have built a house for people and animals, and last fall I had a harvest enough for us and some to sell. I had 87 bushels of wheat and more potatoes than we needed for the year. We also had things from our garden. I had 12 cows, 12 chickens, one dog and one cat, one pig, and one lamb, but I'm not yet owner of this land which my house stands on. It is not so bad, when I can use the land any way I want and receive the harvest and keep animals on it without paying a cent. I will say things are going good.

Here there is green grassland over the whole of America, so if you don't like the place you are staying, you can always find another place. There are many hundreds of thousand miles of land to choose from. . . . We are using the Norwegian language and have Norwegian school and church. There is an English school that is paid for by the state. We must pay for the Norwegian school.

Respectfully, Lars A. Stavig

Nutley

March 2, 1888

Dear Brother K. Stavig,

. . . I hear that people around you in the old country have had good luck and made a lot of money by netting herring. . . .

These days we are sending tickets to my wife's parents and also to her brother, Thomas, if you know him. . . . Greet Berit-Anna Sletten from me and ask her to excuse me for not being able to get a ticket for her until the $300 is paid back.

The family and I are well and they are all around home except Andreas [Andrew, Lars's eldest son]. He is attending English School in the winter and is home in the summer. . . .

Wherever we go in the world, we are tested. Millions come to this country every year, but almost as when we hold a feather in the air to test the wind, so people will experience the sourness of life before the sweet. No one can expect to become independent for the first five years. First, you must work to pay for your ticket and for a place to stay and food. Then, for oxen, wagon and plow before you are ready to start on your own land.

Lars A. Stavig

By the time this photograph was taken in 1889, the Stavig family had grown by four children. In the front row, from left, are Anna, Lars, Peder, Maren, Edwin, and Louise. Standing, from left, are Magnus, Hans, and Andrew. (Stavig House Museum, Sisseton, S.Dak.)

Nutley

August 5, 1888

Dear brother Knudt Stavig,

. . . First, I will inform you that we are fairly well. Maren and I don't feel just right in health or humor, but we must be content with that since we are beginning to be old. I thank the dear Lord Almighty for the young sprouts that are flowering together with us. The children are growing like the field in the springtime. This spring we received another boy child, who is named Edvin [Edwin] Odin. He is a big, good-looking boy. Now there are seven in the family, all at home. . . .

I want you to pay attention to what I'm saying. I lived in Norway for 32 years, and I have now lived in America for 12 years, and I can see the difference. I think you would be doing the right thing by coming to America while you still have the money in hand. It will be too late when you have spent it.

I'm not living in the most convenient place in America, but you must decide where you want to go. Don't decide not to come because you don't like where I live and feel that you have to come here. America also has problems just as Norway does, but there is a difference in their problems. You can be poor in America as well as in Norway. In the beginning it is the worst, before you are situated and have made some money. . . .

Here in this place where I live there is a lot of visiting among neighbors, especially on Sundays. You cannot find many people home on Sunday. There have been many Sundays during the year when we have had 20 people around the dinner table.

Lars A. Stavig

Nutley
November 5, 1888
Honorable brother, Knudt Stavig,

I have been waiting for an answer to my letter that I wrote to you in June shortly after I had received your letter. I told you my full understanding of what you asked me about and if you received my letter you know my feelings. I thought it would be the right thing for you to do to come to America.

We are all well. This year our harvest was fair. I received 1,022 bushels of wheat, 348 bushels of oats, 42 bushels of rye, and 70 bushels of potatoes. The price of wheat is between $1.00 and $1.11. We can't complain about those prices. . . .

Live well in Jesus' name. The friendliest greeting to you and your family from me.

Lars A. Stavig

Nutley
November 29, [1888]
Dear Brother Knudt Stavig,

. . . We are well now as before except for arthritis that bothers me a lot. My son, Andreas, is in town going to school to learn English. He is a good student, and I think if we could afford it he could make something of himself. Hans is studying with the Pastor. Hans and Magnus help me in the barn. Louise Marie and Anna Beata and Peder Olau are working in the house with their mother. This winter we have 24 cows, 11 sheep, and 3 horses to keep in food and water. . . .

Lars A. Stavig

Nutley, South Dakota
August 17, 1891
[Dear brother Knudt Stavig,]

. . . I am glad that you haven't forgotten me with a few lines. I need your brotherly love. I live and we are all well, thanks to the Lord. We are busy with the grain harvest every day now. We are almost through, and the cutting machine works well. The harvest is not large, but good. Almost everywhere in the land the harvest has been good.

Here there are no big changes or much news. They had hail three miles from us, and it ruined their wheat. Some lost everything, and some lost half of their crop. We also had a small hail shower but no real harm to our crop. . . . Greet Mother and your wife from your unforgettable brother. . . .You must excuse my writing. I haven't written anything in a whole year.

Lars A. Stavig

Andrew, also known as Andreas, was the first of the Stavig children to learn English. He posed for this portrait in 1888. (Stavig House Museum, Sisseton, S.Dak.)

Nutley
April 7, 1893
Unforgettable Brother, K. Stavig,

. . . You remember, dear brother, sister, and mother, an evening I was called to your house by Sirianna, my sister, with Ellianna Linnet on her arm. The choke hold that your stepfather had around the neck of my brother, Mathias. Every time I remember it, there are tears in my eyes. In the same way, I remember coming to your help, my dear brother Knut. He had hit you so blood was running from your mouth and nose. I must send my dear old mother my heartfelt thanks for her trust in me to accept her husband's anger. I often remember with a thanks to God that I was able to control my anger and not bring shame and hurt on anyone. . . .

A steam engine with a fuel-tender wagon pulls this threshing machine across the countryside near Nutley in Day County around 1895. (Stavig House Museum, Sisseton, S.Dak.)

Andrew and Magnus are attending school. They are nice kids and stay away from drink, dancing, and card playing. They like to attend school. . . .

I sold eight sheep for a little over $28. Then I sold three oxen for $38. When we sold wheat, we got only 53¢ a bushel. Rye is 25¢ and oats 25¢. To hire a man for 8 to 9 months we pay $210. A girl will work for $2 to $3 a week. What do you think, brother, aren't they fairly good prices? It is more than I could afford to pay. The land where we used to live is going up in price. There is not any land to be had for under $3,000. Where we are now, the land is still low in price. From $8 up to $1,000 for a quarter of a section. A quarter is 160 acres. We must pay $2,200 for a steam threshing machine. They are expensive things that we use in this country to work our land.

If I had stayed in Norway until now, I would probably be able to make enough to live on; that would be all. But now I'm the owner of two quarters of land and a group of good houses, horses, and farm machinery that are worth a lot. My land is worth more than I can ever imagine.[7] I cry tears of happiness many times. Yes, dear brother, we have reason to be glad, when our worth exceeds our greatest expectations.

L. A. Stavig

Nutley, South Dakota
The 7th of January 1895
Dear brother and family,

. . . I have said a lot of things that you might not agree with, but don't worry about that. But I have believed this whole time and it would have been right for you to have left for America instead of settling down at Stavig. . . .

I must tell you that our harvest this year was very good. I had 1,607 bushels of wheat, 700 bushels of oats, 260 bushels of rye and around 7 bushels of potatoes. I got everything thrashed in two days. There were 21 men and we all had a lot to do. We used a steam machine and it went very good. It cost $141 for the thrashing crew, but it really cost us more than that because we had to go to town and buy coffee and sugar for $15 and then I had to slaughter a cow. When we are thrashing it's like a big wedding except we don't use whiskey. Andrew and Magnus are in Minnesota going to a high school there. Hans and I are home tending to our livestock. We have 18 horses, 17 cows, 10 sheep, 3 pigs, 5 turkeys, and 80 chickens, so that keeps us very busy. . . .

We are using coal for heating now. This is our ninth winter in this place. . . .

Lars A. Stavig

Stavik March 15, 1896
Dear brother Lars and family!

. . . Again I have the pleasure to tell you that my family has increased by a child, a boy, who was born the twelfth of March, this month, a very handsome one you can believe. A lot of pleasure for me. All my children are very handsome and attractive, so it is a great pleasure for me to see them. . . .

The weather has been good, so no human life has been lost for four years. But now on Monday, the ninth of March, three men were lost on the sea from Björnsund. It was Halsten Störksen's boat. Two of them were from Björnsund. One married, who had a wife and four children left in poor circumstances. The other was a boy about 16 years old. Sunday he moved to Björnsund, and Monday he passed into eternity. And the third was a man from the fjords around Vogstrand. He was the rower at the Halsten house. He left behind his wife and four children, and his wife also was pregnant and in poor circumstances. The boy from Björnsund was the son of Kristian Clausen, and he also drowned on the sea four years ago[8]. . . .

I can tell you that our brother, Matias, is on track to get married. Anyway, he has a pregnant girlfriend, but I believe he will marry her. She is a fine-looking person, so he can be thankful for the guilt, goodness, and cleverness. . . . I see from your letter that your thoughts are partly here at our house and that you are not free from the thought to come home. Yes, dear brother, let it happen; please come! Come here to us. Think, dear brother, what a meeting it would be! . . .

K. Stavik

Today, the twenty-third, I thought to follow my brother [Mattias] to Molde for a marriage, but nothing came of it, but I believe that it will happen the first.

———————

Nutley
April 11, 1896
Unforgettable brother and family,
Your writing of March 23 was received on April 7th. That letter sure did not take very long. Just think, in that amount of time I or some of you could be visiting each other. When someone from here leaves for a visit to the old home, Norway, I think about taking the trip also, but that will probably never be.

There are different reasons why I can't. First, I have no time since I have only a hired man to help with the farming. The second reason is that the family would not let me take the trip because I'm not so well at times. I might have pain because of my back. The third

reason is that it takes a lot of money that I would have to take away from the family and the farming.

Andrew, Hans, and Magnus have their own land, and they are fairly well. Andrew is buying cows on his own and does business with the stockmarket in Chicago. Magnus is teaching school and is living at home, so he can help me in the evening and morning before he leaves for school. Anna, Peder, and Edvin are home and attend school. Louise is with Hans, her brother. His wife is expecting. For two years in a row, she has delivered a month early, and the babies have died soon after birth. Now we are anxious about how this will go. . . .

You must not send us any herring. It is too expensive. I did not mean it when I wrote. I heard that the fishing had been very good, and so I just wrote it to be funny.

I see something that I really call news. That is our brother, Mathias, is going to get married. I can't believe it's true. I would like to know where he found a woman to suit him. . . .

So live well,

Lars Stavig

Stavik June 20, 1898

My brother Lars!

I am almost ashamed to begin to write to you when it is so long since I last wrote. . . .

I shall tell you that this fall I was on Sandmor with the herring net in Vanelvefjordene. We left from Stavik three weeks before Christmas and came back three weeks after New Year and at the time we caught 2,500 barrels at a price of eight to nine crowns. We had five to six hundred crowns in each share for the use of our nets.

There are many kinds of amusements here now-a-days for young peoples' groups: rifle corps, theatre, and many other kinds of trash and dirt. No, I give thanks that I have my Bible or my devotional book and read the interpretation of the day. The Gospel is much better, I think. I take care of my business in my house with my wife and my children. Dear brother, don't let the Savior's blood have run in vain for us. . . .

[Knudt Stavig]

Nutley

December 12, 1898

[Dear brother Knudt Stavig,]

. . . My work is mostly in the barn. I must feed and water 28 cows, 16 horses, 12 sheep, 7 pigs, and I think about 100 chickens. This fall I sold 8 cows for $185. This summer I cut 150 wagons of hay.

Magnus has also left mother and father and spends all his time with his wife. Andrew, Hans, and Magnus are working together in a store,[9] and it is going well. Four men have more than enough to do in their store. Louise works for them also. We have Anna, Peter, and Edwin at home.

I think I'll quit farming. It is too much for me. . . .
Friendly greetings from your brother,
Lars A. Stavig

Stavik December 1899
Dear brother Lars!
Since these are very busy times for me in many ways, both with the house and with health, I am writing to let you know about my wife. Possibly, you have heard that my wife is sick. She is sick with kidney tuberculosis.[10] Her right kidney is swollen so much that it fills her whole insides. We have now been to three doctors in Bod, Kristiansund, and Molde, but all have said the same thing, that nothing can be done without an operation, and it is very dangerous so that even if she survived the operation, she could die anyway. So, it isn't so good for me, you must believe, who has so large a flock around me of small ones. I have already paid out much money but to no avail. . . . My wife is dying, so I will be alone again with my small ones, and then it is not good to manage alone with a flock of five children.

In the month of October there was a great wonder. People had gathered for herring fishing north in Kristiansund. There were

Lars Stavig stands with members of his family in front of their farm home in Nutley Township in 1900. Lars built the smaller house in the background for the parents of his wife Maren, who also immigrated from Norway. (Stavig House Museum, Sisseton, S.Dak.)

about 3,000 fishermen gathered. There were steamships, fishing boats, open boats and others. They all left with their nets. When they had set their nets a terrible storm came up from the north, northwest and when they should sail home about 250 men were lost. There are many tear-filled eyes to see these days, both married people, parents and relatives. . . .

I have had a desire to see your photograph but I am almost ashamed to say it. Then I myself don't have anything to send you but I shall tell you that this summer I had engaged a photographer Birkeland in Molde to come but he didn't come and you understand that I could hardly travel to Molde with a flock of young ones.

And now when my wife is so sick, I have no portrait of her to give to you, so you could get to see her together with me and my small ones. But I have one of her, which I have gotten. I could send you this, but it is not very good.

She has lost a lot of weight, so it is a sin to see. She has no special pain, so she can lie in peace as far as that is concerned, but I don't dare to say that she will improve again. That, God alone guides and rules over, not I. . . .

K. Stavik

Nutley

December 6, 1899

Dear brother K. Stavig,

I have heard that the people on the Norwegian coast live in sorrow over the big sea disaster that happened around Titeren. We also feel sorrow and loss over the disaster. . . .

. . . I must say that most of us are fairly well, except for my son, Peder, who broke his hip. He has been at the Doctor's for a little over a month. We have brought him home again but he isn't supposed to step on his foot for another month. If it ever heals right I'll be glad. . . .

Andreas, Hans and Magnus have had a business together for five months and they have more to do than they can get done. . . .

You probably know that my wife's parents are living with us. She is 72 years old and he is 82. They are both well and get around. . . .

Lars A. Stavig

The three eldest Stavig brothers, (from left) Andrew, Hans, and Magnus, established the Stavig Brothers store in Sisseton, South Dakota, in 1898. The enterprise would remain in family hands for more than eighty years. (Stavig House Museum, Sisseton, S.Dak.)

Nutley

December 13, 1900

Dear Brother,

It is so long since I received a letter from you that I will write you and renew our brotherly bond. Dear brother, don't let it be long before you write and refresh the old memories. I can still see the old familiar places, and I'm so glad to hear from you. Is mother and your wife still living? How are things with Mattias, Sirianna, and Karen? They are my brothers and sisters, but I never hear anything from them. I suppose it is my own fault. I have also quit writing since I never get an answer.

We are, as usual, fairly well. Except for my son, Peter, who was hurt last fall. . . .

Andrew, Hans, and Magnus, are doing very well in their business. Hans and Magnus have each built new houses this summer. Their houses are 18 feet high and 26 feet square and cost about $1,100 apiece. They are really nice houses. They also have added to their store so it is now 125 feet long and 22 wide, and it is completely full of goods except for one hall. They have seven people working for them, and their business takes in $100, $200, and up to $400 a day. . . .

Hans Stavig is pictured here in the aisle of the brothers' store, which carried everything from pump organs to heating stoves. (Stavig House Museum, Sisseton, S.Dak.)

Wishing you a happy Christmas and New Year. The Lord bless us and all of you in Jesus' name.

I must use glasses when I write to you, and Maren and I have bought new teeth, so the years are taking their toll.

Lars A. Stavig

———————

Stavik May 17, 1901

Dear brother and family!

With a deep sigh I take a pen in my hand in order to thank you for the last writing to me. It is now some time since I got it but I haven't had the will to write before I could see the outcome. I now have the unpleasant news to report to you that my dear Anna died March twenty-first. She wandered from here in the faith in her Savior. This is my great joy in my deep sorrow. You must believe, dear brother, that there is nothing here that gladdens home for me and mine, and the very worst is for my little daughter, Betsy Sofie, who calls "Mama" day and night. It is so heart-rending that I must cry my bitter tears when I hear her call. . . .

Knut Stavig and his family are pictured here around 1910 in a photograph that may have accompanied one of Knut's Christmas letters. From left are Andreas, Beate, Knut, Oluffa, Betsy, and Anna. (Stavig House Museum, Sisseton, S.Dak.)

Andreas Beate   Oluffa Betsy   Anna

Birkeland
MOLDE.

There is something I should have said, but I don't know if I can. But it is, as the man says, the need drives a person to find a wife, and so it is with me also. I can readily say it, also, that I stand in need for money, in order to take care of my family. I don't have much, so I don't know how it will go with us. . . .

K. Stavik

Sisseton
6/14/1901
Knut Stavig
Haronsundet
Relative:
We are including in this letter a bill amounting to 50 kroner, and I think you can get it changed in any store or send it to Trondheim. . . .

This money is from Stavig Brothers.

Nutley, S.D.
July 31, 1901
Dear Uncle,
We received your letter a long time ago and father has wanted many times to write but he has been so busy this summer. . . .

Yes, it was sad that you should lose your wife so soon and have so many small ones. If it weren't so far away we would have taken one of your small daughters and taken care of her for you, but it is so far away that it is impossible. . . .

I hope that these few lines will find you in the best of circumstances and you must write again when you have the chance so we get to hear how you and your small ones live. Yes, greetings from us all and you must greet grandmother also from us. So you must live well.

From your niece,
Louise Stavig

Nutley
October 23, 1901
Dear Brother,
. . . We are fairly well except for Peder, my son, who hurt his hip. I have spent over $400 on him, and he is not well and might be crippled for life. It has been pain and sorrow, but I guess we can't expect anything else. The Lord gives us a cross to bear once in awhile so that we remember to ask God for help. He is the helper of all people in distress and death. I feel compassion for you in the loss of your

wife and also for your little ones. If we were only as close as we are far apart we could have given you some help.

Don't forget to greet old [step]mother if she is alive. How old is she, and is she in good health and satisfied in the world? . . .

Live well.

[Lars A. Stavig]

Stavik November 18, 1901

Dear Brother!

I don't know how to find the words to express myself when I am overwhelmed by good deeds from you. I owe you my heartiest thanks for that which you sent me. It came at exactly the right time. Yes, that is what it did. I stood rightly in a pinch, but now I have enough, so I can straighten myself out for a while. . . . I am still alone with my small ones, and it looks as though I will be alone this winter, also.

. . . You wrote about the possibility of a hired man. I shall enlighten you about that. There is one here who will leave this spring. . . . I have talked with him and he will leave and will come to you if you have use for him and will send him a ticket. Then, he will come to you and be at your house. I have said that it is well possible that you cannot pay what most of them pay, but he is not worried about that in the beginning. The boy is named Peter Hansen Rishaug. . . .

I shall tell you a little about mother. She has been fairly healthy for a long time, but now she is not good. There was a blood vessel that broke in her mouth. It bled many times for two or three days, and so I took her to the doctor. He said that it was a blood vessel which was broken. The doctor would not say that she would get healthy again. She was too old. Now she is fair again, so she putters around with her daily pain. . . . She is soon 70 years old. . . .

K. Stavik

Stavik April 10, 1902

Dear Brother!

. . . In case my former letter doesn't come into your hands, I will herein repeat my request to you. My request is if you could obtain so much money for me that I could pay off my mortgage obligation with Tranen's Savings Bank—about 650 crowns. Against that you would hold a similar mortgage obligation on my farm. . . .

K. Stavik

————————

Nutley
May 4, 1902
Unforgettable Brother,

. . . Before Christmas I received two letters from Norway. One letter from you asking for a ticket for Peder H. Rishaug. The other letter was from Andreas H. Aas, asking for two tickets. I wasn't sure what I should do so I wouldn't offend anyone, but, as I have said before, if someone wants to come over here, I'll send them a ticket. . . . I heard from P. H. Rishaug on 3/2/1902. . . . I received the letter from Peder on March 21 and the 22nd I drove to town and bought a ticket. I bought it from Baarg, and it cost $61.95. May 3rd I received the letter from Peder that the ticket had arrived. . . .

You have to excuse me, but I'm not able to get you as much money as you need without putting my business in jeopardy. Even though we deal in large amounts of money, it comes in and goes out very fast. Last summer I built a warehouse that cost me $700, and I'm paying $40 a month. I also paid $130 for threshing, $50 for taxes, and $40 for coal and wood for the winter. A hired man for the winter is $40. During the summer I hired a man for $170. This year I have a wedding for my oldest daughter May 25. I guess it is high time that I invite you to the wedding. Yes, you must come. I think it would be very entertaining for you. Greet old mother from me and say that she should come for the wedding, too. . . .

Live well in the Lord.

Lars A. Stavig

————————

Stavik December 8, 1902
Dear brother and family!

It almost looks as if the times are becoming worse and worse, so that I don't get time to write a single letter to you any more. But I must now take the time to thank you for Christmas. If my letter will reach you, I don't know. The first thing I will say is that I wish you a merry Christmas and new year. Then, it is a long time since I wrote

In his letter of
4 May 1902,
Lars told Knut
of the pending
marriage of
his daughter
Louise to Andrew
Anderson. (Stavig
House Museum,
Sisseton, S.Dak.)

so I will tell you about the year's happenings. The weather has been very rainy on the whole, the entire summer until fall. Then, it lightened up and since then it has been outstanding fall weather the whole time. The year's crop was not very good. Poor oats and little potatoes and the hay patchy. Fishing has been fair and other things have all been different also. As far as health is concerned, it is good. Old mother is still alive and lives with us. She talks about you often and says that when I write to you, I should greet you with: "You must meet us on the other side of the grave." Yes, we must all wish that. . . .

I will here bring you my heartfelt, innermost thanks, both for the one and the other thing which you have sent me. Thanks for thinking about me and mine. I have wished to get to talk with you, but that will never happen here in this world. But let us meet on the other side of the grave, up there in heaven, at the home of Jesus, who has promised us everlasting salvation. . . .

K. Stavik

Stavik April 26, 1903

Dear brother

. . . As you know, I am alone yet with my small ones. I have no help. I manage the house myself. I see myself often embarrassed and I become tired of all the nonsense that goes on around me, but God shall have thanks. It goes so against, that I don't know about anything. It is God who helps me. Thanks be to God, therefore. Yes, He is my strength and my light. God bless you all.

I shall tell you a little about Erik, north on the farm. He is in fairly good health. He now has gray hair and gray beard, and, as one says, leans toward the grave. Louise, his daughter, has increased the flock of children this winter. She now has her fifth son. Can you believe who is the father? Yes, you remember well three-foot Johan, the tramp who traveled with Engeborg of Pot Ola. Yes, it is he who has been there with her for two years soon. There have been attempts to get him out, but they haven't been successful yet. I could well have much to say about it, but I shall not set myself to it. You can get to know it better with the delivery of this letter.

Hearty greetings from K. Stavik

Sisseton

July 6, 1903

Mr. Knudt Stavig

. . . We recently received the Bible that you sent with Markus Hustad. We must confess that we were very glad to receive such a gift from so far away. We will keep it as long as we live as a reminder of you on the other side of the ocean in old Norway. . . .

We have been very lucky to have had good health almost all of the time. My wife is not always so well but she is feeling well enough to be up every day. My family consists of myself, my wife, and two sons. Our oldest will be five years old on September 5, and the second son will be two years old December 2. Both boys have been blessed with good health. The oldest boy speaks both Norwegian and English very well. . . .

We sent you 50 kroner just before Christmas last year. Did you receive the money?

Magnus Stavig

Nutley Sept. 27, 1903
[Dear brother Knudt Stavig,]
. . . Peder Rishaug became too good for me. He would not work for me for the regular pay. You know he thinks he is big, so the pay has to be bigger, too. I could say more, but I'll wait until another time. I do want to tell you privately, though, that P. Rishaug is not easy to get to know. He does not say many words, but I understand this: if he does not receive our inheritance and marry [our] daughter and rule over everything, he will do us more harm than good. People are strange at times. . . .

The people who come to this country don't know much about work. They can't even feed the pigs. If you need them for a day's work they pull themselves together. In America we must pay $40 a month for a hired man now. After 2 and ½ days there isn't much help from them. . . .

[Lars A. Stavig]

Nutley
January 24, 1904
Brother K. A. Stavig,
. . . I'm now a stranger to all things at home in Norway. I don't see any articles in any papers, and I'm not receiving letters from anyone but you. . . .

I think that when P. Rishaug did not get his way, he let it be known everywhere what kind of people we are. But someone with his spying ways and trickery is not a friend of mine. . . .

We are all well and everything is the same. If you had come to America with me or had come a few years later you would be a rich man now. It could be that you are satisfied with what you have and then you have enough. We cannot take any of these worldly goods with us when we die, but it is good to have a little while we live. . . .

If mother is living, greet her from me.

Lars A. Stavig

Stavik March 13, 1904

Dear brother

. . . I can greet you from mother that she is fairly well, but she is doing poorly. She falls a lot on the slippery floor. She is now both uneven and crooked, so it is risky to have her alone.

I see by the letter that you tell me news of Peder Rishaug. I knew that he thought that way. I heard him talk at times saying that if one of them is married so you have one again. Concerning myself in that regard, I do not feel that way. I think it is best if I am alone.

I have one more idea that I must tell you, but I hesitate to say it. I should forget it, but can't. It is that Louise, north on the farm, is with her sixth child, and it is Trefot Johan again, they say. It must be enough for this time. Greet your sons and daughters from me that I wish them the Lord's blessing. . . .

K. Stavik

Sisseton

April 8, 1904

Dear relative and family,

. . . Father and mother are well and with some hired help are doing as well as before or maybe even better. . . .

This town, Sisseton, keeps on growing and now has almost all the business that older, bigger towns have. We have telephones in almost every house and water for use in houses and for protection against fire. We also have electric lights and other things. There are from 1,400 to 1,500 people living in our town, and they are from many nations. . . . We have a Norwegian Lutheran Church and three American churches. They are Catholic, Methodist, and Presbyterian. Besides that, there are many sects that do not have a church yet. . . .

The family and I are planning on going home for a few days as

FIRST AVE. EAST, SISSETON, S. DAK.

824.

By the time this view of First Avenue East was recorded in 1909, Sisseton was a prosperous community of more than fifteen hundred people. (Stavig House Museum, Sisseton, S.Dak.)

soon as the weather improves. It is not a bad trip when the road is dry. Then, we can drive it in four hours. . . .

So, a friendly greeting to all of you from A[ndreas] L. Stavig.

———

Nutley

July 17, 1904

Dear Unforgettable Brother and Mother,

. . . This summer Maren and I have been on a trip. It is the first trip we have had since we came to this country. We attended the Norwegian Lutheran Church yearly meeting in Albert Lea, Minnesota. . . .

Wasn't it terrible about all the emigrants who lost their lives in the Atlantic Ocean?[11] It's funny when you think about all the people that are lucky and come to America. Where would you find a place for all those people in Norway? The Lord knows and he will lead. I could have said a lot about this, but it is getting to be so late at night that I must quit. It is hard for me to see the letters anymore even though I'm using glasses.

Good night, brother! May the Lord be with us and you in Jesus' name.

Lars A. Stavig

Sisseton

May 3, 1905

Dear Uncle,

I received your letter of April 24. . . . It is very interesting to hear a little once in a while from relatives on the other side of the ocean, where our cradle once stood.

You said that you would wish to be with us, even for a day. That would be my wish, too. I wish you were here so you could see what America is like.

I think that a man who is used to conditions in Norway, where everything is old and built up, would not like it here the first day. You know that our part of America is very new. We are so far west in America that it is only during the last 20 to 30 years that anyone has lived here. Here where we live now was Indian land until about 13 years ago, and up to that time there was no white man living here. Thirteen years ago the Indians—children and grown-ups— each was given 160 acres. The rest of this large land was given to the white man by the government.[12] In this short time almost all the land has been plowed up, houses built, and trees planted. That is a lot of change in such a short time. There is a school house every three miles where the children are instructed in English, history, geography, grammar, writing, reading, etc. Everything is in English, naturally. . . .

In many places people of the same nationality and the same religion try to get land and settle in the same area. But in some places the religion and nationality are so completely mixed up that they will never get a church. If there is no church, there is no Norwegian school either and the children do not have a chance to learn Norse. Then, it will not be long before our mother tongue is forgotten.

Where there is Norwegian, Swedish, Danish, Russian, German,

Polish, French, Indian, and black people in the same community, the English language will be used to make each other understand.

We are lucky to have our own language yet, but it is harder to get our own children to speak it. Lawrence is the name of our oldest son. He is five years old and speaks well in both Norwegian and English. Arthur, who is three years old, will only speak English, but he understands Norwegian well. Little Mildred is only one year old, and what she will speak, I don't know yet. . . .

M[agnus] L. Stavig

Nutley
June 8, 1905
Dear Brother K. A. Stavig,

. . . All of the old die out, and new branches grow on the old stumps.

There probably aren't very many left of the old relatives and friends whom we knew. It is strange to think about the old days. Years come and days go and eternity remains. . . .

I lost the best of my oats last year in a hailstorm. But, thank the Lord, we cannot expect the best of everything. Last year we milked 20 cows and sent the cream to the dairy.[13] We made about $400 from that throughout the year. . . .

You have probably heard that our daughter, Anna, has been engaged to Olle Olson Tornes. He is a son of Berge Olle. They want to send you a picture from the wedding, and it is included in this letter. . . .

L. A. Stavig

Nutley
January 25, 1907
Mr. Knudt A. Stavig,

. . . I'm glad to get a letter from my home in Norway, where my cradle stood and where my eyes first saw daylight. I can see everything before me now. All the roads and trails, inlet and ness, relatives and people we have known, pastors and church. Everything is alive for me from my first memories. Memories of childhood and youth will follow me to my grave. . . .

With his letter of 8 June 1905, Lars sent Knut a copy of the wedding portrait of his youngest daughter, Anna Stavig, and her husband Ole Torness, who were married in December of 1904. (Stavig House Museum, Sisseton, S.Dak.)

Peder Stavig and Tillie London worked together in the Stavig Brothers store and later married. (Stavig House Museum, Sisseton, S.Dak.)

We are getting old now and worn out, so we are not able to do the work ourselves. It is too expensive to hire a stranger to help the whole year around. Our three oldest sons are married and have a store. Our two daughters are also married. Peter works at the store with his brothers. He hasn't been able to work on the farm since he hurt his hip. The youngest son, Edwin Odin, is attending school at St. Olaf. You have probably heard about St. Olaf Choir, which was in Norway last summer.[14] That's the school which Edwin attends. It is the best religious school you can find in America. So, you see, all the children are away. It isn't like Norway, where the oldest son takes over the farm. . . .

Since the children are not here we get lonesome. We will probably rent out the farm and move to town to be together with our children. We will get one half of the crop from the farm if we rent it out and my wife and I can live on that even if we don't do anything.

If I sold the farm I could get at least $8,000 for it, but I wouldn't sell it even if I received a much higher price for it.

Do you think I could have done any better? How do you think I did? Do you think I could have done just as well if I had stayed in Stavik? There are many drops of sweat, many hours of hard work, but the heart has been good the whole time, and we have been lucky, so we have much to be thankful for. . . .

We have had so much snow, wind, and cold that today the thermometer shows 20 below zero. . . . We stay at home when the weather is like this. The wind blows the snow like seaspray, and it reminds me of March 8 so many years ago, when we sailed with the wind and with only the bare mast around Farstadberget.[15] We have had many days like that, when we could barely make it between the house and the granary. It is good to be in America.

Svino [Norway,] December 9, 1907
Dear Uncle!

. . . I shall tell you a little about old grandmother. She is now old and stiff. She cannot walk across the floor in her own strength, and then one is not so good. She has now moved to Uncle Knut and will probably be there the rest of her life. Concerning Uncle Mattias, he is like you, well married and has four children. He has himself a clever wife and has a cozy home. . . .

Anna Beate Svino

On 17 October 1908, Lars's wife, Maren Hustad Stavig, died in Minneapolis, Minnesota, following an operation for gallstones. Left to mourn her loss were her husband and children Andrew, Hans, Magnus, Louise, Anna, Peter, and Edwin. Lars subsequently rented out his land and moved to Sisseton, where he lived with Peter and his wife Tilda. Knut extended his sympathies upon receiving the news.

Stavik March 7, 1909
Dear brother

It is a long time since I have written to you. . . .

The first thing that comes to mind is about the loss of your wife. Yes, I must say that it cuts into my heart when I think back on myself, what I have experienced in this regard. It is difficult to think about; I know myself what it is for anyone to taste—to lose one whom one holds dear. Yes, but God is the one who has to do with this, and, therefore, we have nothing to say about it. It is something which one has to accept. What he—namely, God—does to us, however, is always for our best. . . .

This photograph was the last formal portrait that included the entire
Stavig family. Seated, from left, are Magnus, Lars, Maren, and Edwin.
Standing, from left, are Peder, Anna, Andrew, Louise, and Hans.
(Stavig House Museum, Sisseton, S.Dak.)

Following the funeral of Maren Stavig in October of 1908, Lars (left) helped to lower his wife's casket into the grave using the leather lines of a horse harness. (Stavig House Museum, Sisseton, S.Dak.)

It is often busy for me who am alone in all things. I am now considerably deep in debt. I think between two and three thousand crowns. This is a lot of interest for me each year and especially now when I am not able to earn any money this summer with others. Because of my health, I have not been able to fish for eight to ten years. And it isn't healing very fast. I'm still suffering from a fall I had in church. Each day I feel pain which quickly attacks so I don't know what can come of it. . . .

Brother K. Stavik

Sisseton, S.D.

October 25, 1909

[Dear brother Knudt Stavig,]

Yes, brother, I must gather my thoughts and send you thanks for writing to me and remembering me in my loneliness. At this time I have my home in an upstairs room with my son, Peter, in the town of Sisseton. I pay for my board and room. I'm well, but my loneliness bothers me.

Think, brother, I, who was the father of a large, beautiful family, now sit alone in a room, and it isn't even in my beautiful home. It has been a year full of sorrow, so I have a lot to be thankful for that I have not lost my mind. I'm not poor, but, when you have lost the one who has been your wife for so many years, your happiness turns to sorrow.

To give my thoughts and heart a lift I have been doing some traveling. I had decided to take a trip home to Norway this summer but my company could not go. . . .

The Norway trip was postponed, and the trip will probably never be made. . . .

[Lars A. Stavig]

New Year's Day in Stavik January 1, 1910

Dear brother!

In repayment for the letter, I will send my heartiest thanks for what I have received from your hand. I cannot do otherwise than say God bless you and your sons for what you did for me. It is almost such that I think it is too much for me to receive gifts, time after time, when I am not in shape to move a hand to repay you. . . .

God's Spirit has moved here in our town so that there aren't many homes where there aren't one or more who pray to God. It is a delight to live and to be a witness to such great things that God has done. We have had meetings almost every single day and evening. Last evening we were together for our yearly meeting, and it was good. God's Spirit rests over us.[16]

I see by your letter, brother, that it is sad for you, and I understand it so well. I am experienced in that. . . . I see that you have developed a thought in your mind about seeing your childhood home again. . . . I will say that you should bring the thought up again and come home, dear one. . . .

    K. Stavik

Stavik July 17, 1910

Dear Brother Lars!

Today as my thoughts are directed to you, I will send you a few lines in a short letter so that our closeness as brothers doesn't die out, and, likewise, to tell you that mother is now dead. She died June 14, quietly and peacefully. She was very poorly at the end. The last week she lived, she was not able to talk. We have been relieved of a great inconvenience in my house, but also a great loss, because she was our mother. It is so strange. . . .

    K. Stavig

Sisseton

November 5, 1911

Brother K. Andreasen Stavig,

Your letter written Oct. 10, 1911 arrived here Nov. 3. I thank you. I see from the letter that you would like to see my handwriting and I'm glad. My handwriting is coarse and heavy and that's understandable. First, I'm so old I could be your Father and secondly, my arms have seen very hard work. But I'm glad I have my health and I'm satisfied with my daily work. And it's even dearer than that when the Lord uplifts the heart to give thanks for his guidance, drawing us closer to Him in both the bad days and the good days. Yes, Lord, Father of all grace, our thanks from the inner hearth, soul and spirit for that.

   . . . I hear that there are divisions and conflicts in the church.[17] The time has come when false prophets come to you in sheep's clothing. Sects will attract you to their fellowship and make you a free thinker. It says that the wise will rule the world, and I think that is true. There will soon be a sect for every idea. The Bible is clear about what to do, but you cannot just pick part of the Bible that supports what you believe and ignore the rest. Now our time is full of spiritual teachers who make use of the gift of persuasive speaking ability. . . .

Greet relatives and friends if they ask about me. I'm well, and I have no desire to go back to Norway. Is my old girlfriend, Anne Ols Daughter [V]esta, still alive? It's not the first time I have written her name. Greet her and say I forgive her, and I hope she forgives me.[18] I'll always remember her as long as there is life in me. . . .

[Lars A.] Stavig

Sisseton
January 24, 1913
Brother K. A. Stavig,

. . . It is strange that there is more distance between us but that we talk together as much now as we did before. We are truly brothers in body and spirit and live in the same hope and faith that grace will save us through faith even if it is weak.

I will tell you that I have become weak in my body. I have been to the best doctors in the world and sought healing. I have been keeping myself quiet since I don't have any strength since April 1912, and I am still not good, and I'm not sure that I can be better.

We have removed ourselves from the divisions which they now have in the church. It has harmed both body and soul. I suppose that it can also be a good thing for some. It makes you think over if you really are a branch of the true vine. . . .

You ask about the Stavig Brothers' business. The business is going as before, looked after by the three brothers. They have a lot of help to do the work. There are five clerks that order everything, and they have two bookkeepers the year round. . . .

Lars Stavig

Sisseton
October 28, 1913
Brother Knudt Andriasson Stavig,

. . . Everything I hear from those who have arrived from Norway is that the conditions have improved a lot. That's good to hear. When I was in Norway, there was a large percentage of very poor

Having just arrived from the sea, fishermen in Romsdal fill barrels with herring caught during the winter harvest in 1926. (Romsdalsmuseet, Molde, Norway)

people. What has happened to them is unknown to me. I'm sure that all the motor boats and the improvements in fishing has helped the intake from the large sild [herring] fishing. We didn't have that when I was in Norway. . . . We must pass over and not think about all the grand things you can find these days. We have telephones without wires and aircraft. . . .

If someone would have told us about these things forty years ago, he would have been put in an asylum, and everyone would have thought he was mad. . . .

Lars A. Stavig

Sisseton

February 8, 1914

To Brother Knudt Stavig,

. . . If your daughter wants to come this summer she will have a lot of company. If she doesn't have money for the trip I'm sure that

Lars Stavig, lower right, experienced the novelty of a burro ride on his trip across the United States in 1913. Andrew, at front left, accompanied his father. (Stavig House Museum, Sisseton, S.Dak.)

we can help her out. . . . You must let her come, I'm sure she will like it here. It is best that she makes the acquaintance of a good group to travel with. This summer there are many people from here who are going home and who would give her good company over the ocean. After that the railroad would bring her here and get the ticket for her.

There are always requests for servant girls who are dependable, strong-willed and neat. You probably think I'm bragging, but that is not true. There are always inquiries for servant girls both in towns and out in the country.

It is a long trip from ocean to ocean. I have traveled over the land from the Atlantic to the Pacific. It is a very long trip. It took us many days from New York to Seattle. We traveled on the railroad and had a place to sleep and eat. It was a very comfortable trip. We had a trip on a boat in the Pacific and saw many ships without oars. We also got permission to visit on the boats, and we picked sea shells on the beach and saw the tide. . . . The same year I had this trip west I was supposed to take a trip home, but my company, Hans, was not able to leave home at that time because his wife was expecting. The trip west with Andrew and two others put me out of the mood to travel to Norway. . . .

Peder Kjørsvik asked me to greet you from him. His wife is home running a dance hall. Isn't that nice?

Lars A. Stavig

Stavik June 28, 1915

Dear brother Lars!

. . . I had a letter from Louise this winter and she said you were not feeling well, and, therefore, I will remind you of one thing needful: that you hold fast to the Rock that is Christ.

You are now 71 years old. Your days can soon be counted. When we die, we will be judged. Let us hope that the judgment will be lenient. Then, we will rule with him in eternity. Yes, God grant that I and you and yours and mine meet in heaven at God's house. This is my heartfelt wish for you and me, that God will let this happen in Jesus' name. . . .

This month I was 64 years old so now I'm an old man already. . . .

I don't have any more news to tell you as everything goes in the old Norwegian way. . . .

K. Stavik

[ca. August 1915]
Sisseton, South Dakota
Brother K. Stavig,

. . . In your letter you asked how it is with my soul. I have the best hope and by the grace of God I know I am saved. For a long time I have lived in the trust, faith, and hope. Thank you for the reminder.

I'm not strong in my legs, but I can still get around to my people every day. I'm going to take a long trip of 300 miles to Wisconsin to celebrate the wedding of my baby, Edwin Odin Stavig.

Greetings from all of mine and in the end from me.

Lars A. Stavig

Sisseton, S.D.
Jan. 29, 1916
K. Stavig
Dear Uncle,

. . . First, I'll let you know that my Father is well, and even though he is very gray, he gets around well and does some work in our store every day. He has a room and eats his meals with Peter. On the "gard" or, as we call it, farm, is Olaf Tornes and his sister Inga, and her boy. Tornes rents the farm from Father with the understanding that Father receives half of the crop every year. This has been a good arrangement for both Father and Olaf. . . .

The Norwegian language is used by our pastor at almost all of our morning services, but English is used in the evening most of the time. Our children have learned some Norwegian. The oldest understand Norwegian, but the two young boys speak only English. We are hoping that they, too, will learn both languages.

I should have built a new house this past year, but it is not finished yet.[19] I started in June by moving the old house off from the foundation, as I wanted to build the new house in the same place. It is still not finished, but I hope we can move in in about four or five weeks. . . .

The Andrew and Mary Stavig house in Sisseton is pictured as it neared completion in 1916. Five children would grow up in the house, which is now the Stavig House Museum. (Stavig House Museum, Sisseton, S.Dak.)

Hans is doing fine. They have seven children now, all girls. Brother Magnus has six children. Peder has two and Anna and Tornes have five children. You ask about Edvin. He was married this Fall to a girl he became acquainted with when he attended St. Olaf School. Her parents live in Eau Claire, Wisconsin, and are from Norwegian heritage. Their name is Rusten. I don't know what part of Norway they are from or if they were born in this country. Edvin is in partnership with us other brothers in a store in a new town called Rosholt. Edvin is manager of this store and he has three people working for him. It is 30 miles from Sisseton to Rosholt and we can drive it in 1 ½ hours. It is in the opposite direction from our Father's farm.

Our town that now has about 1,500 inhabitants has put in a sewer system this summer. We also have a new library[20] in the town and a few other new buildings. . . .

A[ndrew] L. Stavig

Sisseton, 27 Sept. 1917
Brother K. Stavig,

. . . I don't suppose I should mention the war and how expensive everything is. If I do, I'll probably get this letter back also.[21] But think, dear brother, what sad times we are living in. A large company of soldiers left from our town.[22] They are our young sons—we follow them to the train as if we were in a funeral procession. Then, we old people are left behind.

I'm sure the Lord in heaven will punish both the bad and the good, so the last day of the world will soon be here and that will put an end to all this misery. We must pray that Lord our God will look in mercy on us and forgive us for this trouble we have caused.

I don't know why, brother, but I could not find peace until I sat down and wrote these things to you. I wonder about that. . . .

L. A. Stavig

Stavik December 10, 1917
Dear Brother Lars!

I received your letter written September 27 on December 7. It had been opened by the censor wherefore I heartily thank them. . . .

I see that there is improvement in spiritual respects. Yes, it is good, because that is what we ought to hold on to. It is from there that help comes, whether we are bad or good. However, most preferably, he (God) blesses us abundantly with undeserved grace, only grace without any deserving of ours. Think, how good God is to us to call us his children. Yes, it would be good if we could call ourselves his little children. It ought to be God who grows and we who decrease. I should tell about how things are coming here among us. We have a lot of revivals in the communities around here. You must believe, dear brother, that it begins to dawn for me, since I now have three of my children who are believers. . . .

I shall tell you that there was one of these evenings that I took up all your letters which I had had from you. It was a pleasant time for me.

K. Stavik

Sisseton

December 22, 1918

K. Stavig

Dear Relatives,

. . . We know that we are well, but the Spanish Influenza[23] is very bad here, and many people we know have died from it.

Father is well. He is back and forth in our town every day. He has been talking about writing to you recently but says he cannot write anymore.

We have tried to build [our store] this year, but it is an expensive time for such work. Materials are expensive, and carpenters and other laborers are asking from $6 to $8 a day. The outside is now completed, and we hope to move into the building in a month. . . .

Four people that we knew, or who had worked in our store, died in the war. . . . Many of our friends are on that side of the ocean and will never return. . . .

A. L. Stavig

Sisseton, So. Dak.

December 29, 1919

To Brother K. Stavig,

. . . I don't have much news, as I seldom get out anymore. Most people speak in a language that I can't understand. I can't keep up with the times anymore. I don't have any desire to write letters; I don't believe anyone can understand me. Everything is strange and has changed. The world reminds me of a frothing sea that can force us to turn in any direction. Everyone wants to be free, free, free. They only want to look out for themselves and don't care what happens to anyone else. There is nothing left of "Do unto others, as you would have them do unto you." Here everyone wants to be boss.

I'm glad I'm so old that I don't have to fight for the Lord's will in the world. I hope there is soon a better place for me.

Wishing you all a Christmas full of blessedness and a good new year. . . .

Lars A. Stavig

Stavik October 21, 1920
Always remembered brother Lars!

. . . This fall I am thinking of giving my farm to my son. He shall have the home farm, and my youngest daughter, Betsy, shall get the inlet there with Skomagernaset, because she has been so faithful toward me. . . . I can also tell you that we have gotten a new minister at Trona again. A young, believing man who is newly graduated from school. He calls himself Sundby, but it is no good to know. He will probably not be here very long, because the reader has already begun to find fault with him for his preaching. It is as can be expected. It can be in our time that ministers are not anything other than radicals who don't preach God's pure word. . . .

K. Stavik

Sisseton, So. Dak.
December 25, 1922
Knudt A. Stavig

This is Christmas Day in America, also, and I have just received a letter from you. Many thanks for the letter. You ask about us and so I'll let you know how we are. Father is in good health and has eaten with us twice today. He was sick last summer, very sick. We thought it would be his last days. But he was well cared for by two doctors and is now healthy again. He is getting old and becoming more forgetful as time goes by. He was 78 years old a few days ago. He goes back and forth in town every day. He makes his home with Peter and eats most of his meals with them. . . .

Even though relatives of children, children's children and children's children's children are so numerous that I don't know them all, yet, I can, after almost 47 years, remember the day we left Norway vividly. . . . There has been a lot of change since the day in 1884 that we moved out here. It took us a week to travel from Starbuck to Roslyn, S.D. We drove with oxen, and we did not have regular roads to follow. Now we can make the trip in 3 to 4 hours, and most of the road is very good gravel. . . .

A. L. Stavig

Stavik February 15, 1923

Much Loved Brother Lars!

. . . I don't know if it is enough that I thank you seven times. I think truly it must be unto 70 times seven times and yet more. I don't know how to fully thank you for what you did for me, because now I have gotten the bond in my hands, so the risk is prevented. I will tell you how I came into this pinch. I was naïve enough to co-sign for my son and my daughter's husband, Arne Jacobsen, for this amount. The monthly sum was not paid and so the bank demanded that I should pay the bond with a mortgage on my farm which I did. I did it for their sake. I work much harder compared with them. I can tell them that I only have enough to take care of myself. . . .

God's peace be over you all in Jesus' name is my wish.

K. Stavik

Sisseton

February 19, 1923

Old honorable brother, Knudt Stavig,

. . . You have been the one who has kept me informed of how things are in my motherland, the place where I walked in my child-hood, youth, and early manhood, the place I will not forget. I re-member all the roads and trails I walked from the mountains to the seashore. So, if I'm very inquisitive as to how things are going, you must pardon me.

I had no high school to learn in. The only school I had was a ro-tation school. We spent a week at each farm with a long table—the length of the room—the children crowded around and a school-master. . . . That was all the learning that I had.

Last summer I was very sick. I guess I was near death. I had two doctors who attended me, and they did not think I had any chance of surviving. I have not been my old self since then, but I thank God for each day that has passed. . . .

Many of my grandchildren are at Northfield attending school and studying different things: some to be pastors and others to be doctors and professors and lawyers. The women are learning all crafts. . . .

I'm sending you a small gift, but it is too small to be of much help. Live well. Wishes from brother,

Lars A. Stavig

Stavik March 26, 1923

Unforgettable dear brother Lars!

. . . In regard to intake here, there is more going out than coming in. As far as I know, I am done with farm work. I want to quit and let my son take over the work hereafter. I believe that I told Andreas of my plans for the fall. I have gotten God's promise to be healthy, and it is an overwhelmingly great mercy. . . . This isn't a long letter, but just so you can see I'm alive. . . . God's grace and blessing be manifold upon you.

K. Stavik

Sisseton

January 22, 1924

Dear Brother Knudt,

I thank you for the letter you sent me. It is good to know that you received the letter with the money and have gotten your farm paid for. It makes my heart feel good. . . . I will give you some ideas of what I would do if I were K. A. Stavig and owned my own farm. I would give my son, Andreas, a free deed to the farm without having him pay anything to his sisters and brothers. He probably does not have anything to start with anyway. This would give him an incentive and he would see that there would be a future for him there. He would help himself and his father who has been alone so many years with his sorrow and his happiness. I know for myself that when your wife is gone, there isn't much of a home left for the husband or children. When I think back, my heart is full of sorrow and I have tears in my eyes. Not that I'm in need of anything in either body or soul, but mostly because I sit here alone. I know you will say I have my children around me. They are my trust and my happiness, but I must mention that when the language is strange, it is not much comfort. . . .

Lars A. Stavig

Lars Stavig was photographed on a sidewalk in Sisseton some years after he rented his farm and moved to town to live with his son Peder. (Stavig House Museum, Sisseton, S.Dak.)

Aas [Norway,] February 12, 1924

My up in years brother

. . . I have heard that you have helped Knut. Our magnificent God bless you and repay you for your compassion. He has worked hard alone for his children, but he is a man. I almost thought to tell you a word, but it is best to be silent; then, I am safe. You know well that they were kind to our old Mother. Poor Mother, who cried so that they could hear her out on the road. Oh, yes, yes, to cry for your children looks bad. I have more than half of my nine children in the grave; yes, so it is.

Sirianna Aas

Sisseton

April 12, 1924

Brother Knudt,

. . . Yes, dear brother, I will admit my poor, honest stupidity that has filled me. If the Lord in Heaven had not been my taskmaster . . . [only] with God Almighty's guiding, I am what I am today. . . . I have had three years of hailstorms on my farm, and the fourth year I did not get enough to pay taxes and nothing to keep the farm in good repair. . . .

You ask what your sister [Sirianna] knows about me. . . . I remember it as if it happened this night. [Sirianna] came through the door with Mas Anders in her arms, screaming that I must come at once and help. I ran to the house that stood on the old foundation, and I found you on one side of Knute Ellingson, and my stepmother on the other side, holding him against a cupboard, and K[nute] Ellingson had a chokehold on Mattias' neck, so that he had fainted. . . .

I must admit that even now I have tears in my eyes, when I think back over the situation. It will follow me to my grave. It wounded my heart. . . .

So, in the end, live well.

Lars A. Stavig

Sisseton

November 1925

[Dear brother Knudt Stavig,]

A friendly thank you for the letter I have received but it is becoming much harder for me to answer. I have started many times and then put it away. I have lost so much of my memory that it is almost impossible for me to think of anything to write. . . . I'm getting to be too old to keep up with the times. I'm one who cannot understand the language, and it is especially bad in church.

I have been sick for a while, but I'm feeling a little better now. I was 81 years old November 21st, 1925, and I do believe my life's work is over.

[Lars A. Stavig]

Sisseton

January 15, 1926

Brother Knudt:

I will try again to send you a few words to thank you for the letter and the good news. Yes, brother, isn't the world inventing some interesting things? While I'm sitting here writing to you, I can hear the radio coming through the air right into our house. There is music and talk every day in America and even from as far away as Germany. . . .

[Lars A. Stavig]

Stavik October 19, 1926

Dear brother!

I have waited a long time to hear from you but nothing has come so I feel it is my duty to send some words to let you know what is happening. Our dear sister, Sirianna, died on October 15. On the twenty-first she will be buried in Vaagöe churchyard. She has not been well for many years. She was bedridden for only eight days. Yes, now her work is over. . . .

Greetings to everyone from me, your brother.

K. Stavik

Sisseton
February 20, 1928
[Dear brother Knudt Stavig,]

It is over a year since I wrote a few words to Norway. I have let Ole Mathiassen Stavig do it for me. . . . He is a good writer, but if he gets a letter he doesn't tell me about it.

Not everyone in America is living among the flowers. There is a lot of sorrow here and a lot of poor people. America looks good. There are a lot of expensive cars in heaven but only very poor people on earth. Everyone wants to be important, and they don't care about anyone else and are not willing to help anyone. They demand high wages. Can the world exist under these inconsistencies? It is good the Lord still gives us a period of grace. . . .

Here are a lot of new things that I don't understand. I don't understand the English that is used both by church and state.[24] It is lonesome for me when I don't understand my own family. . . .

Lars A. Stavig

Wearing his fisherman's cap, an aging Knut Stavig posed for this picture taken in Norway around 1925. (Romsdalsmuseet, Molde, Norway)

Sisseton
February 2, 1929
Brother K. Stavig,

. . . The world has really changed. It has become very strange. Is it us, or is the whole world coming apart? What do you think, brother? Is it just me with my hearing loss? It sounds like a rumbling noise or like the noise at the mill when you are grinding grain. I can remember everything about all that is old. My childhood and youth I remember the best. I suppose that means that I'm getting old. I don't know so much about what is happening in day-to-day life. I can't understand the preacher and especially not people in the house, since they have started to speak English.

I have actually lost my good sense. I sit within four walls and have only two windows facing toward town, and they are frozen over with ice. I have lived in this same room for 20 years—ever since I came to Sisseton. I guess I should be happy and content, since I have my children around me, but they have not been feeling well. Andrew has high blood pressure, and Louise has cancer. My daughter, Anna, has recently come home from Minneapolis, where she was operated for gallstones.

I must be happy and thankful and content with how the Lord leads us and brings us home to himself in the end. He will keep His promise if we pray about it in love. He who has gone ahead to prepare a place for us will pray for us. . . .

Lars A. Stavig

Stavik March 11, 1929

Unforgettable Dear Brother!

I send you my best greeting and thanks for the letter which I have received recently from you from which I see that you are thinking about me and have not forgotten me. . . .

I understand that everything from your childhood days comes into mind. I don't know if I should awaken your memory or not. I was in Bud lately, and then I spoke with Anne [Vesta, Lars's old girlfriend.] She has now become old and gray. The bloom of youth is withered and gone. Anne was fairly healthy. Don't get mad at me for telling you this. . . . Yes, you have a desire to know my work. I have quit everything, both large herring and cod fishing. My present work is to sew shoes and sea boots, a little farming. . .

Knut Stavik

Sisseton, December 1929

[Dear brother Knudt Stavig,]

. . . . I'm tired of this world and wish to rest on the Lord's happy shore, where there is no change any more. I can't understand the English language, so everything is lost for me—happiness and sorrow. I feel I have nothing to live for any more. I was 85 years old November 21. . . .

I wish all of you a Merry Christmas and a Blessed New Year.

Lars A. Stavig

A cyclone went through my farm and blew down my barn—or granary, as you call it in Norway—and the chicken house. Everything was twisted and broken, and all the trees were uprooted. It was sad to see. Especially, for me, who had worked so hard to get it into the shape it was. It was a wonderful home, brother, if you had seen it before it was damaged. It was such a happy place for me that I must brag about it. . . .

Stavik January 5, 1930

My always remembered brother and family

I received your much welcomed letter of December 6, 1929. . . . I see in your letter that an illness has hit you, and that wasn't very good for me to hear. . . .

I see in your letter that Peter has lost his one son. I feel with them in their sorrow. . . .

K. Stavik

Sisseton

November 20, 1930

Knudt Andreason Stavig

Tornes, Norway

Dear Uncle,

It is almost Christmas and I have been thinking about you. I'm sending you the amount of 81 kroner that I want you to divide among the relatives. . . .

Today is the 20th of November, and father will be 86 years old tomorrow. He is well and gets around but stays in the house most of the time. . . .

Andreas L. Stavig

Sisseton, S. Dak.

December 9, 1930

Dear Uncle,

. . . Father is fairly well for his age. He was 86 years old on November 21. All the children gather every year for his birthday—the pastor always comes and gives a talk and says a prayer. It's always a nice time. . . .

Louise

Lars, now infirm and needing almost constant attention, was moved to the Hans Stavig home, where Hans's wife Pauline was able to offer capable nursing care for him. At the same time, he mourned the death of his daughter, Anna Stavig Torness, who died on 27 January 1931, leaving a large family of young children.

Sisseton
Dec. 13, 1932
[Dear brother Knudt Stavig,]

I thought I would write a letter to you to thank you for the last letter you sent. I received it on the day I was 88 years old—the 21st of November.

Hans finishes the letter for Lars, who was too weak to continue:

That was all he thought he could write. He has been bedridden for 18 months. He is not so sick, but he is not able to stand or walk. He has a good appetite. . . .

He worked for 1/2 day to write those lines. He said to tell you he thinks these will be the last lines from him. My wife takes care of him. . . . We had him out for a drive a couple of times this summer. We carried him out to the car. He likes to go for drives and to smoke his pipe as usual. . . .

I will tell you he has all his senses and lives in the Lord. . . .

Lars Stavig

[Sisseton] Sept.19, 1933
Dear brother of my father,

I'm writing a few words to you to let you know that our father and your brother has been taken home to his Lord. He died on July 27 and was buried on August 1. He was sick for almost a week before he died peacefully in his sleep. Prior to that, he had been bedridden for almost two years. My sister, Louise, died a month before my father. She had cancer. That makes two in our family who have left us this summer. It fills our hearts with sorrow, but we must be

thankful and glad for the hope that we will meet them later in company with God.

    Hans L. Stavig

After the death of Lars Stavig, correspondence continued from the family in America to Knut, especially from Magnus Stavig, and his son, Lawrence.

Following several years of declining health, Lars Stavig died at the age of eighty-eight in July of 1933. Here, the Stavig sons and other mourners gather at the graveside following his funeral. (Stavig House Museum, Sisseton S.Dak.)

Sisseton,

Oct. 22, 1933

Dear Relatives,

    . . . The times are very bad here. We have never experienced anything like this before. Millions are without work and without money to buy the necessities of life. Food and drink enough for many years for all of us, but nothing to buy it with.

    It is not easy to think what will happen. Many think that people will not die from hunger without a rebellion. God knows what will happen. It is probably good for us that we cannot see what the future will bring. . . .

M. L. Stavig with family

———————————

Sisseton
March 18, 1934
Dear Uncle and other relatives,

. . . We are experiencing strange times. The prosperity and wealth which was so common is now no more. People who were rich or well off a short time ago cannot now earn their bread. Millions are out of work, but we must remember that it will get better. . . .

M. L. Stavig and family

———————————

Sisseton, S.D.
March 12, 1935
Dear relative Knut,

. . . A deep sorrow and huge loss has struck us this winter in the death of our brother, Andrew. . . .

When we lost Andrew, it was the worst loss of all. He was the one who had been our leader. He showed us the way. He broke the ground. We just followed in his footsteps. When we followed in his footsteps we were sure that we were on the right track. He lived a life that will not soon be forgotten. He was loved and looked up to by everyone who knew him. . . .

There are strange times ahead. For 51 years we have lived here in the same place in South Dakota, but never before have we had a year like the one that just passed away, 1934. Not a straw for hay, no potatoes, and no crop of any kind. Hay is close to $20 to $30 for a load. That is 80 to 120 kroner. It will take three loads to feed one cow for a winter, and that means that it would cost $400 to feed one cow for a winter.[25] In that way, no one would be able to keep their cattle. They would sell or give them away or let them die from hunger, as many of them did. Thousands of cattle were shot and buried, hide and all.[26]

Magnus Stavig

Two years later, Magnus made the trip back to Norway in the company of his son, Pastor Lawrence Stavig. Just before Christmas 1937, Lawrence wrote to his great uncle Knut.

St. John's Lutheran Church
Northfield, Mn.
December 10, 1937
Dear Uncle Knute,

There have been many days since father and I traveled from Molde and Romsdal after having had such a delightful visit with all of you. Many, many times I have thought about sitting down to write, but I have never found the time to do it. But now I will send Christmas greetings to all of you. I will use the opportunity to write some lines in addition. I find it easy when I talk with you face to face but it goes more slowly and with difficulty when I try to write. If the truth be told it is because of my deficiency in writing Norwegian that I have not written before. But now I must try and you must excuse my many mistakes.

You will never know how much happiness the opportunity to come to Norway and, especially, to Stavik, gave us. . . .

We often marveled over your strength and power, that you could travel with us day and night—and you a man of over 80 years. . . .

When I left Bergen, over the ocean to England, it was almost as if I was leaving my home. I looked back toward Bergen's mountains—Norway's coast—and felt the tears come to my eyes. . . .

Lawrence

The next decades brought death to the remaining members of Lars's family. Hans died in 1946; Peter, in 1960; Magnus, in 1962, and Edwin, in 1965. Knut Stavik died in Norway in 1950 at the age of ninety-nine.

Perhaps the greatest legacy of pioneering immigrants like Lars Stavig was to give to their descendants the will to endure and the strength to overcome calamities like the Great Depression and World War II. Like the very lives their authors lived, the letters of Lars and Knut Stavig reflect the hardships faced by families in both Norway and America and give voice to the indomitable spirit of those who pioneer.

NOTES

1. Møre og Romsdal, called Romsdals Amt in 1876, is one of nineteen counties located on the western edge of southern Norway. The county covers an area of almost fifty-eight hundred square miles with forty-seven hundred miles of coastline facing the Norwegian Sea. The county is divided into thirty-six municipalities. Fræna kommune (Fræna community) is the area in Romsdal from which Lars Stavig left for America. "More og Romsdal," http://mrfylke.no/Om-Moere-og-Romsdal/Moere-og-Romsdal.

2. Lars Stavig is writing about the new town of Starbuck, Minnesota, which would supplant White Bear Center. A community of mostly Scandinavian immigrants, Starbuck was formally platted in spring 1882 and incorporated in 1883. The Lake Traverse & St. Cloud Railroad (a subsidiary of the Great Northern Railroad) and the Little Falls & Dakota Railroad (associated with the Northern Pacific Railroad) competed to reach Starbuck first, with the Little Falls & Dakota winning the contest and gaining the mail franchise for the town. The line would

also have hauled Lars's wheat even though the community did not have an elevator until several years later. Odd S. Lovoll, *Norwegians on the Prairie: Ethnicity and the Development of the Country Town* (Saint Paul: Minnesota Historical Society Press, in cooperation with the Norwegian-American Historical Association, 2006), pp. 133–34; Carmen Tschofen, "National Register of Historic Places Nomination Form: Little Falls and Dakota Depot," May 2005, sec. 8, p. 4, Pope County Historical Society Collection, Glenwood, Minn.; Gary Richter, *Starbuck, 1883–1983* (N.p.: Starbuck Study Club, Centennial History Book Committee, 1983), p. 53.

3. Tax records show that Lars owned three cows, three one-year-old calves, two two-year-old calves, and two other cattle over three years old, likely oxen. He also paid tax on one wagon and one clock. The value of all property as determined by the assessor was $209.00. Personal property assessment, Township of White Bear Lake, Pope County, Minn., 1882, Pope County Historical Society, Glenwood, Minn.

4. The party likely traveled west along the Wadsworth Trail, established in 1864 as an improved military road between Saint Cloud, Minnesota, and Fort Wadsworth (later Fort Sisseton), about thirty-five miles west of present-day Sisseton, S.Dak. Minnesota Highway 28 generally follows the Wadsworth Trail from Starbuck to Browns Valley, Minnesota. A stone marker just west of Browns Valley off Highway 28 marks the Wadsworth Trail near the location where Lars Stavig would have crossed into Dakota Territory on his way to the homestead just north of present-day Roslyn, Day County, South Dakota. Grace Cynthia Hall, *The Wadsworth Trail* (Morris, Minn.: By The Author, 1938), pp. 5–7, 41–42; *Day County History* (Webster, S.Dak.: Day County Historical Research Committee, 1981), pp. 17, 357; "Canku-Cahdephi Footsteps on the Trail," museum exhibit, Stevens County Historical Society Museum, Morris, Minn.

5. Rowing for fish, as Knut calls it, required a team of eight men in a heavy wooden boat using long wooden oars to row out into the Norwegian Sea, usually during the winter months of December through March when fishing was best. The men wore goatskin coats, the outside of the hide having been rubbed with tar and codfish oil to make it more water resistant, and leather boots that came over the knee with knob-nailed wooden soles for traction. Casting and hauling in fishing nets was strenuous, dangerous work. The men carried no life preserving equipment, and a capsized boat would leave them in freezing water wearing heavy clothing. After a long day rowing for fish, there were nets to repair in their small fishing huts, where the beds were stacked one above the other. They slept two men to each bed in order to stay warm during the cold winter nights. Interview with Mads Langnes, Romsdal, Norway, July 2010.

6. A Norwegian mile is equal to about 6.2 miles in the United States. It was used as a unit of measurement before Norway adopted the metric system in 1889. "Scandinavian Mile," *Wikipedia*, en.wikipedia.org/wiki/Scandinavian_mile.

7. Lars had been required under the Homestead Act to pay the United States

government $2.50 per acre for his original claim, and the land he homesteaded had increased in value by almost 200 percent. The two quarters of land Lars owned were composed of the original homestead and timber culture (tree claim). In 1908, tax records for Nutley Township indicate the assessed valuation of the land to be $1,191 for the tree claim in the E1/2 SW1/4; NW1/4 SW1/4; and Lot 1 of Section 28, and $1,053 for the original homestead in the S1/2 NW1/4; SW1/4 NE1/4; NW1/4 SE 1/4 of Section 28, Township 124 North, Range 55 West of the 5th Principal Meridian in Day County, South Dakota. Register of Deeds Office, Day County Courthouse, Webster, S.Dak.

8. The fishing community of Bjornsund was in a group of islands located at the inlet to the Romsdal Fjord facing the Hustadvika, a dangerous stretch of the Norwegian Sea between the communities of Bud and Hustad, where the waves crash onto the rocky, unprotected Romsdal coastline. At the time Knut was writing to Lars, there would have been several hundred people living on the three main islands of Bjornsund. Since 1971, no one has lived on the island, and the homes are used only for holiday. "Fræna municipality, Møre og Romsdal, Norway," *Wikipedia*, en.wikipedia.org/wiki/Bj%C3%B8rnsund. In his memoir, Lars wrote of another fishing disaster that occurred when a large storm, or hurricane, as it was called in the *Romsdal Budstikke* newspaper, hit the coast on 8 March 1871. (Lars incorrectly recorded the year as 1872.) During winter's peak fishing season, each boat would have carried a fishing team of eight men. The church book of Aukra parish, the parish neighboring Fræna, lists the names of sixteen men, or two fishing teams, from this single parish who died in the 1871 storm. Other records indicate that one fishing team from Fræna and another one from Hustad also died that day. Most of these men were between twenty-five to thirty years old, still in their prime years. Lars A. Stavig, *Memories* ([Sisseton, S.Dak.]: By the Author, n.d.), p. 6; Mads Langnes, Konservator, Romsdalsmuseet (Romsdal Museum), email to author, n.d.

9. Andrew, Hans, and Magnus Stavig established the Stavig Brothers general merchandise store in Sisseton in 1898. The store became a prominent fixture on Main Street and well known throughout the area. It remained a family enterprise until 1983, when new owners took over. Norma Johnson, *Wagon Wheels: A Collection of Stories about People, Places, and Events in Northeastern South Dakota*, vol. 5 (Sisseton, S.Dak.: By the Author, 1986), pp. 7, 82.

10. Kidney tuberculosis is caused by the same bacteria as tuberculosis of the lungs. Left untreated, it can cause the kidney to become calcified and ultimately stop working. Weight loss is a common symptom. John B. Eastwood, Catherine M. Corbishley, and John M. Grange, "Tuberculosis and the Kidney," *Journal of the American Society of Nephrology* 12 (2001): 1307–14.

11. On 28 June 1904, the Danish steamship *Norge* hit Saint Helen's reef off Rockall, an uninhabited island west of the British Isles, and sank with approximately 620 passengers and crew members on board. The ship had left Kris-

tiansand, Norway, on 25 June with 727 passengers and a crew of 68. Norwegian newspapers printed accounts of the shipwreck, poems, and obituaries. Bjørn Davidsen, "They Faced Death at St. Helen," digitalarkivet.uib.no/utstilling/eng/dsnorge.htm; "Rockall," *Wikipedia*, en.wikipedia.org/wiki/Rockall.

12. The Lake Traverse Indian Reservation in what is now South Dakota was established by treaty on 19 February 1867 and terminated as part of the Indian Appropriations Act of 1891. The act not only opened all unallotted lands to non-Indian settlement but also appropriated to the Sisseton and Wahpeton Sioux a $2.50 per-acre payment for the unallotted lands, which the government then sold to non-Indians for the same price. *Erickson v. Feather et al*, 420 U.S. 425 (1975). *See also* Michael L. Lawson, "Indian Heirship Lands: The Lake Traverse Experience," *South Dakota History* 12: 216–19.

13. At the Nutley Township Creamery, which opened in 1904 or 1905, workers skimmed cream off of cooled milk and made it into butter. The creamery ultimately closed due to competition from surrounding towns. *History of Day County*, pp. 334–35.

14. Lars is slightly confused on this point. The St. Olaf Concert Band played in Molde on 13 July 1906 before a crowd of about one thousand people. It was not until 1913 that the choir made its first trip there. Paul G. Schmidt, "The 1906 Band Tour to Norway," *My Years at St. Olaf*, www.stolaf.edu/collections/archives/scripts/myyearsatstolaf/6.html.

15. Farstadberget is the name of a farm with a hill, or a headland, on the mainland where it projects out in the Norwegian Sea just north of Farstad, Norway. Lars again recalls the March 1871 storm when the men in the boat would have dropped the sails and let the boat drift until it came around Farstadberget into the safety of the bay of Farstadbukten. Inland from the bay is the community of Farstad, which lies at the base of Stemshesten, a mountain that rises more than two thousand feet above sea level. Visible from the Norwegian Sea, Stemshesten has for centuries been a landmark for navigation. "Stemshesten," peakery.com/stemshesten; Department of Informatics, University of Bergen, "The Top 100 Mountains of Northern Norway Ranked by Prominence," www.ii.uib.no/~petter/mountains/Norway/norway_finestmap.html.

16. Norwegian author Edvard Hoem grew up in the Fræna municipality of Romsdal, where his family has lived for generations. Hoem related that his grandfather, also a farmer/fisherman, became "a convinced believer [who] found it to be his duty to do something to spread the gospel," and later collected money for his prayer house at Hoem. Lay preachers would hold meetings several times a week for the fishermen and fish-packers in Bud and Bjørnsund and conduct "*vekkelse*, where hundreds of fishermen went down on their knees, confessed their sins and 'gave their heart to God' as they often termed it. This is the kind of religious activity that Knut writes about to Lars." Edvard Hoem, email to authors, 19 Feb. 2012. For more on these lay preachers who followed in the evangelical, revivalist tradi-

tion of the famous preacher Hans Nielsen Hauge (1771–1824), see Hoem's essay, "One Family, Two Lands: Why Did We Leave?," in this volume.

17. The Lutheran church in Norway experienced turbulence in the late nineteenth and early twentieth centuries. Much of the conflict revolved around "liberal theology," which had its roots in scientific studies in America and Germany concerning the reliability of the Old and New Testaments. Nobel Prize-winning author Bjørnstjerne Bjørnson (1832–1910) was an aggressive spokesman for the new ideas. His strongest opponents were Johan Christian (J. C.) Heuch (1838–1904), Norwegian bishop and politician for the Conservative Party, and Jacob Sverdrup Smitt (1835–1899), a Norwegian bishop and politician. Hoem, e-mail to authors, 19 Feb. 2012; "Banquet Speech: The Nobel Prize in Literature 1903, Bjornstjerne Bjornston" *Nobelprize.org*, www.nobelprize.org/nobel_prizes/literary/laureates/1903/bjornson_speech.html#; "Johan Christian Heuch," *Wikipedia*, en.wikipedia.org/wiki/JohanChristian_Heuch.

18. A passage in Lars's memoir sheds light on this statement: "Short engagements and quick marriages were uncommon in those days. It was customary to be engaged for several years. For three years I went regularly to see Anne Vesta every Saturday night when it was possible. I loved her and she loved me and we firmly believed we were intended for each other. It was customary in Norway to get the consent of a girl's parents before you were married. I sent a man [named] Ole Strand to my girl's parents to ask for their consent to marry their daughter. I did not know that this Ole Strand had himself tried to win the heart of Anne Vesta. As could be expected under the circumstances, they refused to give their consent" (Stavig, *Memories*, p. 4). As a result, she married neither man.

19. The home then under construction is the one that Andrew's daughter Mathilda later willed to the Heritage Museum of Roberts County and now stands as the Stavig House Museum in Sisseton.

20. Sisseton's Carnegie Library opened on 16 March 1916. The Carnegie Corporation promised $7,500 if the city council would pass an ordinance guaranteeing at least $750 in annual support. Voters accepted Carnegie's proposal and the city council approved the ordinance. *Sisseton Weekly Standard*, 17 Mar. 1916.

21. Postal censorship or inspection during World War I allowed the government to open mail and read the contents of letters, selectively obliterating sections deemed potentially harmful to the war effort or returning entire letters to the sender. At least one envelope associated with a letter from Knut to Lars dated 27 September 1917 has a white label resealing the opened envelope and reading in English, "Opened by Censor 5089." Stavig Letters, acc. no. H2010-052, State Archives Collection, South Dakota State Historical Society, Pierre.

22. The *Sisseton Weekly Standard* published a list of over sixty men leaving for military duty on 5 July 1918. Each man's name was preceded by his military service number.

23. Eight people died of influenza in Roberts County between October and December 1918, while statewide the flu accounted for 28 percent of total deaths

for the year. To avoid contagion, church services were suspended, funerals were held outdoors, and other public gatherings were prohibited. "A vast majority of the 1,847 flu related deaths [in 1918] occurred in a three month time span. . . . It appears you had two outcomes if you contracted the flu—either you died within three days to a week or you lived" (Matthew T. Reitzel, "1918 Flu Pandemic in South Dakota Remembered," history.sd.gov/Archives/forms/spanishflu/Spanish %20Flu%20Article.pdf).

24. When Lars Stavig homesteaded in Nutley Township with other Norwegian-speaking families in 1884, the Norwegian language was used in the home, in church, and to conduct business. In 1917, the Goodwill Lutheran Church in Sisseton began conducting worship services in English every other Sunday and eventually discontinued the Norwegian-language service altogether. Local government and business affairs were also conducted in English. Eventually families began to speak only English in their homes. Art Torness, a grandson of Lars Stavig, recalled, "I never heard him speak a word of English" (interview of Art Torness, Sisseton, S.Dak., n.d.). *See also* Norma Johnson and Oliver Swenumson, eds., *Across the Years: History of Sisseton, South Dakota, 1892–1992* (Sisseton, S.Dak.: Sisseton Centennial Book Committee, 1992), pp. 140–41.

25. Perhaps Magnus meant that it would cost four hundred kroner to feed one cow for the winter. At thirty dollars per load and three loads needed, it would actually cost ninety dollars for feed.

26. During the 1930s, more than 75 percent of the United States experienced drought and in twenty-seven states, the drought was considered to be severe. Combined with economic depression, the effects were catastrophic. Cecil Stagman of Sisseton was fourteen years old at the time and recalls that hundreds of cattle were herded into pens at the north side of town. Farmers received twelve to twenty dollars per head, depending on weight and condition, from the Drought Relief Service program of the federal government. Once the cattle had been herded to the edge of a large pit, they were shot, rolled into the pit, and covered with dirt. The hundreds of red metal tags they had worn were saved on a wire that stretched taller than a man. Cattle in other areas were destroyed in the same manner. "Timeline: Surviving the Dust Bowl, 1931–1939," www.pbs.org/wgbh/ americanexperience/features/timeline/dustbowl; interview of Cecil Stagman, Sisseton, S.Dak., n.d. For more on the Dust Bowl in South Dakota, *see* Gerald W. Wolff and Joseph H. Cash, eds., "South Dakotans Remember the Great Depression," *South Dakota History* 19 (Summer 1989): 224–58.

One Family, Two Lands

Why Did We Leave?

EDVARD HOEM

While on a visit from Norway to Sisseton, South Dakota, more than twenty years ago, I showed two of my father's second cousins, who are distantly related to the Stavig family and whom I had met for the first time, a photograph of an old farmhouse. This home in Norway was the one that their father, also named Edvard Hoem, had left with his parents and siblings in 1886 when they emigrated to America. My South Dakota relatives looked at each other and simultaneously exclaimed, "Why did they leave?"

The reasons why nearly one million Norwegians left their homeland to go to America during the nineteenth and early twentieth centuries are more than complex. Historians cite causes that differ between the "inner" (events inside Norway) and the "outer" (events and pressures from outside the country). A majority of those who emigrated first were families—parents with children, who sometimes took with them their own parents. They looked for land to settle on and cultivate, where a family house could be planned and realized; a place where fellow countrymen had already arrived, where a school could be built and a church could be founded. Many in this first generation of settlers spoke their mother tongue as long as they lived and could hardly make themselves understood in English. As time passed and a new century drew closer, young, unmarried women and men in their twenties became a significant emigrant group. They learned English rapidly, forgot their background, went to the cities, and merged into modern American society, losing contact with their emigrant fellows as well as their homeland.

Why did they leave? Historically, Norway had been an undeveloped outskirt of northern Europe that existed under Danish rule for more than three hundred years. After the Napoleonic wars (1803–1815), Norway was given as a prize of war to Sweden under the Treaty of Kiel, signed on 14 January 1814. Sweden's pretender to the throne, the French general Jean Baptiste Bernadotte (later called Karl Johan), ruled over both countries, but Sweden played a leading role in this alliance. Humiliated, the Norwegians joined Christian Frederik, heir to the Danish throne, in an uprising. A constitutional assembly was held in Eidsvoll in central Norway in the spring of 1814, and a constitution proclaiming independence, inspired by the French and the American constitutions, was signed on 17 May. Sweden sent troops into Norway in the summer of 1814, and, after a short war Christian Frederik, whom the constitutional delegates had elected King of Norway, resigned and returned to Denmark. The royal union of Norway and Sweden was established on 4 November of the same year.[1]

For the next ninety years, the Norwegian people would oppose Swedish rule to varying degrees, claiming the rights of the Eidsvoll constitution of 1814. During this period, the Norwegian Parliament, or Storting, passed many important legislative milestones in a sort of extended, peaceful revolution that gradually took power from the hands of the king's officials and placed it in the hands of the people. Among this milestone legislation was the establishment of municipal councils and municipal self-government in 1837, the granting of school education for all children in 1860, the founding of the supremacy of the jury in 1887, and the common vote for all men in 1898 (women received universal suffrage for all elections in 1913). Thus the struggle for national independence and a democratic Norwegian society were joined in a dynamic process, which finally led to the dissolution of the union on 7 June 1905.[2]

Not everyone could wait that long for change, however. Some of the first Norwegian emigrants who left the city of Stavanger with the sailing ship *Restauration* in 1825 were religious dissidents, the Quakers. Another group on board was the Haugeans, followers of the lay preacher Hans Nielsen Hauge (1771–1824), a peasant's son who, in the spring of 1796, received a calling to spread the gospel among the common people. According to the Conventicle Act of 1741, laymen were forbidden to preach without the consent of

Hans Nielsen Hauge challenged the authority of the established state church, and some Norwegians emigrated to the United States for religious reasons. These followers of Hauge's teachings are assembled in front of the Norwegian Mission Prayer House in Stavik, Norway. (Romsdalsmuseet, Molde, Norway)

the local parish pastor. But while Hauge wandered from district to district in southern Norway instructing people on how to build sawmills and obtain salt from sea water, he also preached in the evenings, gaining the confidence of those who gathered to listen. Hauge even let women stand up and give their testimonies in these house meetings.[3]

Hauge's evangelical preaching was a challenge to state and church authorities, and he was arrested several times and eventually imprisoned in 1804. The prison conditions were so hard that his health was broken by the time he gained his freedom in 1811, but his spirit lived on among thousands of followers for one hundred fifty years. They rarely called themselves Haugeans and were not members of any formal organization, so it is difficult to know how many of Hauge's followers went to America, but their numbers on the emigrant ships must have been considerable. In the 1840s, hundreds of Norwegian emigrants went to Muskego in southern Wisconsin, where the Haugeans strongly set their imprint on society.[4] Modern historians of emigration reasonably suggest that earlier historians have underestimated the Haugean influence on emigration. The Haugeans remained a strong factor in Norwegian religious life until World War II.[5]

Another strong "inner" factor prompting emigration was inspiration from the February Revolution of 1848 in France, which turned so many things in Europe upside down. The emigrant numbers show the effect of this impulse. In 1842, some 500 emigrants left Norway. In 1849, the numbers grew to more than 4,000. Altogether, 36,070 people left Norway for the United States during the 1850s, or an average of more than 3,600 persons per year, according to official statistics. An important inspiration in these years came from the famous master fiddler Ole Bull (1810–1880), who tried to establish a Norwegian settlement in Pennsylvania called Oleanna. His utopian effort failed, however, and he returned to Norway in 1857.[6]

Another influential personality who encouraged emigration was the leader of the first socialist movement in Norway, Marcus Thrane. As a young man, Thrane (1817–1890) had wandered around Europe for several years. French authorities eventually returned him to his homeland, accusing him of vagrancy, and he began working as a journalist in the city of Drammen, close to Oslo. His articles addressed the political situation on the European continent, including the February Revolution. In 1849, he traveled all over southern Norway, establishing workers' associations and a radical newspaper. Economic depression in the late 1840s led to a serious food shortage among those at the bottom of the social hierarchy. Thrane organized more than thirty thousand men, demanding that the import customs on grain be removed, as these customs hit consumers hardest. He also demanded improvement of the public schools and advocated general conscription, not the compulsory military service that only fell to poor people and the sons of peasants who could not afford to pay their way out of service. Thrane's most important demand, however, was the common vote.[7]

The Thrane movement grew so strong that the authorities in Norway sought a method to crush it. Among Thrane's opponents were the majority of church officials, who accused the free-thinker of blasphemy. In July 1851, when Thrane and other group leaders were gathered in Oslo, the police arrested 147 men, including Thrane, who were later sentenced to hard prison terms. Thrane was released in 1858 and left for the United States a few years later, encouraging sympathizers to join him. A closer analysis shows that most members of the Thrane movement did not come from the lower classes of cotters and other poor people. In accordance with the general trend in emigration, most of them were craftsmen, many of them carpenters and sailors, and not the poorest members of society.[8]

I hypothesize that the moving force behind the first wave of Norwegian emigration to America was the Haugean movement and the February Revolution, but not in the sense that the emigrants were all strong believers or revolutionaries or socialists. The revolution in France challenged and brought into question the legitimacy of the ruling order. A spirit of freedom was in the air. People felt that spirit, even as the uproars of 1848 were beaten down all over Europe. When quick political change seemed impossible, people looked for an alternative. Many emigrants, when asked, reported conflicts with local officials among their reasons for leaving. Common people claimed the right to decide what was best for themselves and not to be told so by the clergymen and lawyers who, first and foremost, feathered their own nests.

An unrest in the heart led the majority of those eight hundred thousand people who left in waves from all parts of Norway between 1825 and 1925 to seek a better life in the promised land. They were utopians in the sense that their opposition to the official church had given them a taste of something else. Poor economic conditions, the lack of land, or the desire for a stable income put the question of emigration on the agenda. The final decision to leave was made in the hope of finding something better for themselves, for their children, and for future generations.[9]

The story of emigration is a crucial part of Norwegian history. Critical voices among the authorities, as well as among writers and intellectuals, denounced the emigration, claiming it took away the best of the country's youth and intellectual capacity. The emigrants were accused of being adventurers and vagabonds looking for easy money. Those who stayed home soon realized that they had better living conditions, more land, and more jobs to share, but the improvements had a price. Families were split up; parents never saw their children again; siblings and other relatives never reunited. The emigration story is a chronicle of loss and distance.[10]

The immigrants in America wrote tens of thousands of letters to their relatives and friends in Norway, letters that wandered from hand to hand and inspired new groups to break away and leave. This volume contains correspondence between two half-brothers, Lars Stavig and Knut Stavig, who grew up on the Norwegian west coast in the latter half of the nineteenth century.[11] Lars Stavig, born in 1844, emigrated to America with his wife and three sons in 1876, while Knut Stavig, born in 1851, decided to stay on the farm where they grew up. The letters they exchanged over a period of fifty years do not give us any specific reason as to why one brother decided to leave and the other chose to stay. As the letters show, they were close friends, but the Stavig family relations were complex.

Stavig Bay, the birthplace of Lars and Knut, is situated on the Fræna fjord halfway between the cities of Bergen and Trondheim, about ten miles from the little town of Molde. The trading and

Olaf Mahles Motor Slip Bud.

Boats lie moored at the trading and fishing village of Bud, which became one of many hubs of activity in western Norway during the winter fishing season. (Romsdalmuseet, Molde, Norway)

fishing village of Bud is a few miles away, and closer is Harøysund, home to the medical officer of health. He was the only doctor in a wide area. The sheriff had his farm a couple of miles away, at Tornes. Another name that occurs several times in the correspondence is Bjørnsund, two small islands some miles off the coast from Bud, where many farmers went fishing in the winter season. The roads were miserable in most places, but they improved little by little during the 1850s and 1860s. Local steamships were to be seen on the fjord beginning in the late 1850s, passing to and fro from Molde and including Tornes, Harøysund, and Bud on their routes. Paradoxically, the building of conveniences like railways and the steamships that traveled the fjords and lakes increased emigration rather than encouraged residents to stay.

I was born in 1949, more than a hundred years after Lars, on a small farm in the same area where Lars and Knut had lived. Although conditions were far better and the economic situation for farmers on the Norwegian west coast had improved over the ten

decades between Lars's birthday and mine, there were many simi-
larities in the lifeways and traditions of Lars's time and those of my
childhood years.[12]

The advent of World War II delayed the development of water
power in my homeplace, and for the same reason electricity did not
reach these neighborhoods until 1953. Lack of money prevented the
farmers from buying modern agricultural machinery, and farming
remained old-fashioned hard labor. Like me, Lars probably learned
the art of reading by the light of a kerosene lamp. Perhaps he, too,
could remember the great shadows, caused by the lamp, of a mother
moving back and forth in the kitchen.

In my early childhood, cars were seen on the roads daily, but
the horse was still an important draft animal on the farms, as they
were when Lars departed in 1876. In my time, many farmers left
their families in the winter to join the seasonal herring fisheries,
when the "silver of the sea" came swimming by the millions towards
the coast. In Lars's and Knut's time, fishing was a part of daily life.
The people of the Norwegian west coast survived through the classic combination of fishing and farming, many of them staying for
weeks or months on the islands of Bjørnsund during the winter.

Living conditions were hard in Norway in the middle of the nineteenth century. The eldest son of the farmer was considered the
lucky one because he had the allodial right to the farm, a tradition
that has been practiced from time immemorial. Even if the farm was
sold to someone outside of the family, the eldest son could put forward a claim and buy it back within fifty years.[13] The other children
would find work as craftsmen, field hands, maids, servants, or as
cotters, who would rent land from a farmer, build a house or a hut,
and pay for the rented ground by working for the landowner. The
number of cotters in Norway increased until the mid-nineteenth
century, reaching their peak in the late 1850s.[14]

It was also common for siblings to share their parents' land and
practice a combination of farming and fishing in the local fjords.
The sharing of farms might have been a reasonable short-term
solution, but it had a negative outcome as the farms became too
small to feed expanding families and later delayed the purchase
of modern agricultural equipment. My relatives in the Sisseton,

South Dakota, area left Norway because two brothers, Ola and Erik Hoem, decided in 1876 to share a farm that was once considered one of the best in the area. To give the younger brother, Erik, a place to stay, the farmhouse was extended to accommodate two families. The older brother, Ola, mortgaged the house for one thousand Norwegian kroner—at that time a considerable amount of money—to make the addition possible.

In the meantime, Erik became a carpenter, married, and decided to build a new house of his own some hundred yards away from the main farmhouse. When Ola ran into economic difficulties during the early 1880s, a difficult period with cold summers and bad crops, he could not afford to pay the interest on his loan. One day while working in the field, Ola realized that the bank could take his farm. He thrust his hoe into the ground with great force and declared that he wanted to go to America. In reality, he had no choice. Ola was more than forty years old and had three small children—Bastian, Edvard, and Sanna—when he left his allodial farm. A fourth child was in her mother's womb when they left from Bergen on 18 May 1886.[15]

Erik had no means to buy Ola's farm. The brothers arranged an auction and sold the farm to redeem the mortgage loan. The new owner might have known that his takeover could be risky should Ola's eldest son return from America, assert his allodial right, and claim the farm. The risk, however, was limited. Those who came back were the exception, proving the rule that those who left left for good. One such exception was the author and Nobel Prize-winner Knut Hamsun, who in his youth lived in the United States twice. Hamsun worked as a clerk at a store in Wisconsin, as a streetcar conductor in Minneapolis, and as a field hand on Oliver Dalrymple's bonanza farm in North Dakota before he returned to Norway and became famous for his book *Sult* [Hunger], written and published in Copenhagen in 1890.[16] Hamsun was a forerunner of other single young people who left for the United States and later returned with the money they had made to start anew in their fatherland. When entire families emigrated, however, they rarely returned.

Ola did not leave at random. His sister Hjertine, who had told the parish pastor upon her confirmation at age sixteen that he was teaching a false theology, had left for Roslyn, in what would become South Dakota, some years earlier with her husband Ole Aas, a saddle maker. The Aas family was related to the Stavig people through Lars's sister Sirianna, who had married a man from the Aas family in Norway. Ola's mother, Ingeborg, was born in Stavig and was also related to Lars. Ola settled on the Dakota prairie in the vicinity of Fort Sisseton. In 1895, he was kicked by a horse and died, but his sons and daughters were neighbors of Lars Stavig in the Sisseton area, and their descendants still live there.

The emigration wave came late to the district of Romsdal, situated near the Trøndelag region of central Norway. Lars was among the first who went away, and twenty years later, hundreds of people from the area were leaving every year from the harbors of Bergen, Trondheim, Kristiansund, and Aalesund. Local newspapers became common at this time, and although many people could not afford to subscribe, they could borrow copies from wealthier neighbors and read about life "over there." Until 1870 or so, Norwegian sailing ships brought the emigrants to America. Later on, steamships took over and emigration became an important business for English shipping companies. The Allan Line was one of the English ship lines that established offices in Trondheim and Bergen. Agents from the steamship companies went from town to town in Norway offering tickets that would take the emigrants all the way to their final destinations in Minnesota or Wisconsin. More than four hundred sixty thousand people left Norway for the United States in the last four decades of the nineteenth century.[17]

The year 1876 was one of high emigration for the people of Romsdal, especially those from the municipality of Fræna where the Stavig brothers had their home. Although economic depression in America reduced the numbers of emigrants overall, the stream of people from the Romsdal district increased. Those who had already settled in Minnesota and other places in the United States wrote letters back home praising the new "Promised Land" to prove to themselves and others that they had done the right thing in emigrating. Although life in the new world may have been hard, it had something to offer that the old world was lacking: possibilities, hope, expectations, and enough land to create a better future. In 1876, twenty-four persons from Fræna emigrated to America.[18]

It was not easy to say goodbye to close relatives and good friends and sail away towards an unknown world. Some of the emigrants borrowed money from relatives and neighbors, only to pay it back years later. Those who left in 1876, as Lars Stavig and his family did, went by steamer to Bergen, where they boarded a steamship, possibly from the Allan Line of England. After arriving in Quebec, Canada, the most common destination in those days, the early immigrants would travel down a series of waterways towards the Great Lakes and cities like Chicago, Illinois, or Milwaukee, Wisconsin.[19] Later immigrants like the Stavigs ventured on into Minnesota, making much of the journey by rail but concluding it in Dakota Territory by wagon or on foot. Many of the immigrants survived their first year in dugouts and sod houses. Despite the poor conditions, most immigrants had no other choice than to stay until their last days, probably with "the land where their cradle once stood," as Lars Stavig sometimes referred to Norway, on their minds.

What did these immigrants leave behind? Norway in 1876 had about 1.8 million inhabitants, most of whom were farmers and cotters. The population of Norway was increasing rapidly, passing one million in 1822 and two million in 1890. In the last three decades of the nineteenth century, the capital of Oslo (at that time called Kristiania) became a city of more than two hundred thousand inhabitants, with industrial enterprises and active trade. Ironically, the development of industries, the building of roads and bridges, and the growth of steamer traffic all seemed to stimulate emigration instead of reducing it. Many people first went into the cities to get jobs and earn money, but after a few months or a couple of years they moved on to America. Gradually, Norway changed during the late 1800s and early 1900s from an agricultural society with a barter economy into an industrial society.[20]

But in 1876, the year Lars Stavig left for America, life in the rural areas of Norway's west coast was the same as it had been in the seventeenth and eighteenth centuries. Electricity, indoor plumbing, and motorized transportation were unknown phenomena to the fishermen and farmers who lived there. Change had started, but it came slowly. A trip from Romsdal to Kristiania took more than two weeks. The first railway was built from Kristiania to Eidsvoll in 1844. Steamers on the fjords and lakes did not become common until the 1860s.

The farms on Norway's west coast were small and relied on hard manual labor. The farmers in Lars's time had one—and rarely more than one—horse, maybe three or four cows and cow-calf pairs, one oxen, and perhaps a dozen sheep and goats that fed in the mountains and on the moors for most of the year. The climate on the Norwegian west coast is rainy, and in winter the storms come frequently, but because of the Gulf Stream the temperature does not fall far below zero degrees Celsius, or thirty-two degrees Fahrenheit. A typical farmstead might have had several houses, a barn for the hay with a cowshed underneath, and sometimes a stable and a sheepcote. Last, but not least, on the beach below the farm stood a boathouse with a *færing*, a four-oared boat about twenty feet long, and a larger *åttring* with four pairs of oars, mainly used when the farmers went to the banks out at sea in the fishing season, or as a transport when they went to church on the other side of the fjord or on visits to Molde or Kristiansund. The boat for daily use was the *færing*, which could be maneuvered by one or two men. Most farmers were also pretty good sailors, aware of the fact that a storm might rise suddenly when they were at sea, so they watched the weather carefully. The coastal sea nearby, Hustadvika, was particularly dangerous with thousands of underwater rocks. Especially in the winter, fishing could save the coastal population from hunger.

Most Norwegians knew how to read and write, but rarely did they have books other than a hymn book and maybe a Bible. The people of Norway were largely Lutheran Protestants, many of them strongly influenced by the Hauge religious awakening of the early nineteenth century. Following the leader Hans Nielsen Hauge's direction, the Haugeans rarely broke away from the Lutheran church establishment even though they maintained that the religious teachings of many of the clergy were not in accordance with the word of the Bible. Haugeans stressed the importance of individual religious life, daily divine service, and the Lutheran thesis of the

common priesthood, which maintains that every man and woman is a priest before God. They organized "house meetings," where they sang, prayed, and shared with their neighbors their personal witness about how they had found salvation.

Let us try to enter into the daily lives of these people in the different seasons of the year. Although the winters could be mild and the snow might disappear early, agricultural work could rarely start before late April or early May. The first task was to take the animal dung from the barns out onto the fields and then plow, harrow, and plant potatoes. Barley was the most common crop grown in the cool, wet climate, although oats could ripen if good weather extended into the autumn. The cattle were driven out from the cowhouse in mid-May and would be left to wander fairly widely. In some cases, the farmers built summer cow sheds and milked the cows where they were grazing. The sheep would graze for months alone in the mountains, sometimes with one or more shepherds — young men who would scream and shout to frighten away any wild animals, be they wolves, bears, or lynxes, that might turn up. In the late nineteenth and early twentieth centuries, such animals were not common, but they existed.

When the plowing and sowing season was over and the cattle were left to seek their food in the mountains, it was time to dig peat in the moors to use as fuel during the long winter. In the Middle Ages and before, enormous oak forests covered the Norwegian coasts,[21] and peat is the partially decayed organic material such as leaves, bark, and moss that have accumulated through the centuries. Workers removed the grass and heather on the surface of the peat moors and then dug out pieces of the moist mold beneath using a special spade. The size of a brick, the pieces would be dried in the sun and put together in small "stacks" that were easy to pick up for loading onto sleighs in the snow. Sleighs were even used in the summer because wheel carriages were expensive and used for transporting heavier goods.

With the winter fuel thus secured (those who had forests, of course, would cut down trees for wood to burn), it was time to cut the hay and leave it to dry before bringing it safely into the barn. The hay was scattered by the female members of the family when the morning dew had dried, then put together in small ricks before the dew formed again. Another method for drying hay was to hang it on a rack. The hay season used to be a busy time, and often the whole family joined in the work. Hired field hands might be brought in to help, along with young maid servants, called outdoor maids. The maids slept in the attic, the men often in the barn, making their beds in the hay. Some places had a second harvest of hay in late August, but on the coast it was more common to leave the later growth for the cattle to graze for the rest of their outdoor season. During the first part of the summer, the days are very long in the area where the Stavig farms are situated. In the precious mid-year weeks of June, people may sit outdoors reading a book all through the night. Starting in late July, however, darkness returns earlier every evening, and with the darkness comes wistfulness and the acknowledgement that summer will soon be over.

The farmer in 1876 had no time for sadness or melancholia. All summer he had a net in the bay, for he was a fisherman as well as a farmer. He inspected his nets every morning, and now and then he caught a cod or a haddock and had fresh fish for dinner. At times, the fjord might suddenly boil with huge numbers of pollock, and the farmer would run to his boat and row out with his sons to catch them. The sea fed and saved these people when the crops failed, which they often did because of the unstable and rainy weather. Although food was often scarce, many of the fishermen would throw away mackerel because, it was said, that fish fed on the remains of drowned sailors. One of the sons might do the rowing, while the father and another youngster threw out lines; the pollock would bite willingly at the baits, sometimes several fish at once. Another day, the fishermen might conclude that the sea was empty. When successful, they brought the fish back home and stored them with salt in wooden barrels.

While the men were fishing, the female members of the family went to the moors and the mountains in July or August to pick the abundance of blueberries, mountain cranberries, and cloudberries, which were the most important source of vitamin C, a necessity that people in Lars's and Knut's time knew little about. In some places during the last decades of the nineteenth century farmers planted fruit trees—this area had plum trees and apple trees—but it was difficult to save the ripened fruits when flocks of birds came in to take them. Bananas, oranges, and pineapples, as well as other fruits from southern Europe and Africa, were still unknown to the fisher-farmer's children.

In the beginning of September, it was time to harvest the potatoes, which were fundamental to the fisher-farmer's diet. Potatoes became common in Norway in the first part of the nineteenth century and, some say, saved the growing Norwegian population from starving. The potato may, in fact, have been part of the reason why the population increased so fast, the abundance of nature resulting in the contradiction of poverty among the common people. When families dug their potatoes, they sorted them into three different wooden crates: the big potatoes were for sale, those in the middle were for their own consumption, and the small ones were saved as seed potatoes for the coming spring. To keep the potatoes from freezing during winter, they were stored in the stone cellar of the house. Vegetables were rare, but certain foresighted farmers in 1876 may have grown carrots and turnips on small portions of their land.

The fisher-farmer in 1876 had his first meal early in the morning, as early as four or five o'clock in summer, and he went to bed at nine in the evening. In winter, the whole family went to bed early to conserve the sheep's tallow that was used in the lamps and lights. In earlier times, they had to use a *kole*, a sort of cup that hung from the ceiling and was filled with fish oil and furnished with a wick of woolen thread. Kerosene lamps became common around the time Lars was born, but still the inhabitants of Stavig were obliged to go to bed when darkness fell because kerosene was too expensive to be used.

In October, it was time to bring the sheep back from the grazing land on the mountain, a task that might go on for days. The women of the family cut the wool and all through the winter sat at their spinning wheels making thread and yarn for weaving and knitting clothes of all kinds: wool scarves and gloves and homespun frieze for shirts and pants. Some people also had silk scarves and waist-coats, bought in Molde or Kristiansund, or even in the faraway city of Trondheim, which a common man, if he was brave, might visit once or twice during his lifetime. Some of the men had hats, and those from the upper classes, of course, had robes, jackets, and coats made from animal skin, camel hair, and imported fabrics, but everyday clothing was made from the material that people produced themselves. Often, even shoes were handmade from tanned oxen hides by the local shoemaker, who walked from house to house, ate with the families, and slept in their beds until he had finished his work. While the women would spin and weave, the men, when they were not stopped by bad weather, fished throughout winter. Hundreds of men gathered in Bud and Bjørnsund, catching cod and salting it in barrels to be sold at markets all over Norway.

People worked intensively six days a week from dawn till night. On the seventh day, they might take the *åttring*, which could easily carry a dozen people, and row to the local church to listen to the service. Children went to school three days a week. During Lars's childhood, the school was ambulatory, with teachers going from farm to farm, teaching in the living quarters of one farming family for two weeks before moving on to the neighboring farm. The first Stavig school building was raised in 1886. Lars never saw it, but Knut's children went to that school.

Change was coming, but slowly. As education improved and the art of reading became common, people's eyes opened to the possibilities of a new world. The burden of tradition also encouraged family rebels to escape. From their early childhood years, children had to take part in the work on the farm, herding the cows and sheep at the summer pastures, digging potatoes, and feeding the animals in the barn through winter. It was not regarded as proper to oppose parental authority, even when it came to grown-up affairs like marriage. When a young man desired a bride, he sent a matchmaker to the girl's parents, but the marriages were not entirely arranged. A young girl had the opportunity to say yes or no after the parents had given their consent. It was easy for a farm owner to find a bride, as he was considered able to feed a family. The bride's future as a farmer's wife on those small farms was not a bed of roses, however. She had to join her husband in hard work. Milking was the duty of the housewife, and she fed the cattle when the men were fishing at sea. Still, those who had a piece of land were better off than those who were cotters and worked for the landowner.

The expected life span was about sixty years for men, a little more for women. Frequently people died in their prime, at age thirty or forty, from tuberculosis and other common diseases. Because it was hard for a family to survive when one spouse died, remarrying was common, and young men might marry widows who were twenty years older. In turn, a widowed man might remarry and beget children with a far younger wife. Such was exactly the case with the Stavig family. Lars Stavig was born 30 November 1844. His father, Andreas Lasseson Stavik, had married Marit Alvsdotter Vestavik, a widow with five children, in 1842, and the couple had one child together—Lars. Marit died when Lars was one and a half years old, and her two eldest sons died, as well. The widower Andreas now was left with Lars and three stepsons.[22]

Andreas got the allodial right to the Stavig farm, called Knutgarden, by a king's deed of conveyance in 1845, which also gave his children the allodial right to the farm.[23] Andreas then married

Brit Knutsdotter Haukas, who was eighteen years younger than he and who became stepmother to Lars and his half brothers. Brit and Andreas had five children, giving Lars five more half siblings! Lars's half siblings would gain the allodial right in order of age, if Lars denounced it. Andreas now had nine youngsters to provide for. The three elder and the five younger were not related to each other, while Lars was half brother to them all. As the eldest son of Andreas, Lars inherited the farm when his father died in 1853 at the age of fifty-five, but in order to take over the farm he would have to pay a sum of money to each of his younger half siblings.

Lars's stepmother Brit then married a man named Knut Ellingson, who was seven years younger than she. According to the law, Lars was obliged to give accommodation and support to Brit and Knut for the rest of their lives, although neither of them were his parents. Because Knut Ellingson was still a young man, Lars faced the possibility of having to accommodate him for decades. In this way, the keeper of the allodial right, who should have been protected by this extremely old practice, was brought almost to ruin. Lars had to find a way out.

Initially, it appears that Lars wanted to stay on his allodial soil, but because he could hardly do that without a wife, he wanted to marry Anne Vesta, who had been his betrothed for three years. In keeping with custom, Lars sent a friend of his to her parents to ask for their consent, unaware that the friend also wanted to marry Anne. Exactly what happened next, nobody can say. Possibly Lars's friend betrayed him. Or maybe he first asked on Lars's behalf and was rejected and then asked on his own behalf and for the parents' permission to marry Anne. She, however, did not marry either man. Eventually, Lars married his domestic maid, Maren Hustad. By the time they left Norway in May of 1876, they had three sons together: Andreas (Andrew), born in 1869, Hans, born in 1872, and Magnus, born in 1874.[24]

After Lars left his allodial farm, his stepfather Knut Ellingson gained the deed of conveyance on the Stavig farm in 1877. He did not have any allodial right, but his stepson Mathias did, as second in the order of succession. Mathias had a lung disease, possibly tuberculosis or asthma, and never ran the farm. He turned it over to his brother Knut, the half-brother of Lars, who eventually got the deed in 1888.[25] Knut was born in 1851 and died in 1950, close to his ninety-ninth birthday. This man is the Knut Stavig who corresponded with Lars Stavig for forty years.

Lars had not been well off in Norway, but he was not starving, either. According to the census of 1865, he had a horse, four cows, seventeen sheep, and a pig. The census of 1875 indicates that he had two horses, four cows, two calves, eight sheep, a goat, and a pig on the farm.[26] The stock was sufficient to feed a family, so why did he leave? Most likely he made the decision to emigrate because of the long-term prospects and lack of possibilities for his three sons. Only one of them could inherit the farm, and that event might not come to pass for fifty years. There is no obvious reason why Lars should leave and Knut should stay, no convincing explanation, but one: Lars's spirit of adventure and his ability to make the difficult final decision to leave for the new world.

Lars Stavig was aware of the dangers that awaited him and his family. He must have heard of the Indian uprising of 1862, when more than six hundred white settlers were killed by the Dakota Sioux. On the other hand, there were dangers in Norway, too, especially at sea. He had survived the sudden, catastrophic storm of 8 March 1872, when about forty fishermen had drowned. Another important reason for leaving was that both of Lars's surviving elder half-brothers had the same intentions. Early in 1876, the three eldest Stavig brothers started selling everything they could not bring with them. Homemade trunks and caskets were packed, and it was time to say goodbye.

Lars did not make his decision to emigrate in isolation. Rather, his family was part of a group of related families that set aim for the new world. In addition to the families of Lars's elder stepbrothers, several members of the Aas family joined, too. Some years later, my relative Ola Hoem left, encouraged by his sister Hjertine, the wife of Ole Aas, who had settled in Roslyn, South Dakota. A picture of Hjertine's house in Roslyn is in my possession, found among the things that Hjertine's brother Erik, the carpenter, left behind when he emigrated.

There ends the Norway chapter of the emigrants' story. Several members of the same families, mostly young people, joined the group in the Sisseton area. Two of them were nephews of Hjertine and cousins of Ola's children. One of them went back to Norway and bought a farm in Molde. Another one, my great-uncle Eilert Knutson Ræknæs, went to Canada when the Alberta prairie was opened for settlers, probably in 1902.

The correspondence between Lars Stavig and Knut Stavig was followed by letters from younger relatives who frequently asked Lars for a ticket to America, promising to work hard for him or another employer to pay back the money. Other family members in Norway also asked for financial support. Even Knut, who now owned the family farm, had to ask his half-brother for financial assistance, which he never paid back. He had a bank loan but lacked money to pay the mortgage. One year, Knut earned one hundred kroner for the salmon he caught in a net in the fjord. That was good money. Bad weather, however, frequently prevented him from going out fishing and getting a good harvest, and Knut was too old to follow when the most progressive fishermen started buying larger boats with motors. These fishermen hunted herring in a greater area and went further out into the North Sea. Knut stayed at home and reported in one letter that he had harvested ten barrels of potatoes, which just was enough to feed five people through a year; subsequently, he had little for sale. Ten years later, Knut built a millhouse to grind his barley, but the project was never completed. More and more, his letters to Lars deal with religious matters.

As the Stavig correspondence shows, Knut became more and more a strong religious believer, filling up the letters with traditional Haugean modes of expression. He joined in the prayer meetings where "awakened" neighbors came together to kneel down, confess their sins, and ask for grace and redemption. The "friends," as they often called themselves, started to collect money to build a prayer house in the Stavig area, and a prayer house was consecrated in the 1890s. Lars was worried when he heard from Knut that there was much religious confusion in the church congregation. The Haugeans obviously had no confidence in the new parish pastor in Vågøy, who, in Knut's eyes, was a radical who did not proclaim the

true word of God. The Haugeans worshipped in their prayer house and went to church more rarely, as they practiced their own communion. Some of them wanted to form a new sect, and they ended up rebaptizing each other in the Tornes River. Hauge himself had personally warned against such sectarian tendencies almost a hundred years earlier. In Hauge's time, his followers were the forerunners, building sawmills and extracting salt from the sea. Now, they were more and more suspicious of all new thought, such as Darwin's theory of evolution and women's rights. The religious truths that had been a living reality in Hauge's time turned into a stale phraseology that seemed strange to those who did not belong to the group. As happens with most reform movements, it degenerated from openness into dogmatism and narrowmindedness.

Even so, for fifty years and more, the Haugeans were a mighty group within the Norwegian church, and their imprint on the democratic movement in nineteenth-century Norway can hardly be overestimated. They opened a direct line from the individual person's longing heart on earth to God's listening ear in heaven. They confessed their sins and had to beg on their knees for grace and forgiveness, but they believed Christ would raise them up so they frankly and happily could be his witnesses among their fellow citizens. Eventually, they would stand before Christ's throne with their emigrant friends and relatives and praise him eternally. Knut's letters are an excellent example of this late Haugean spiritualism.

In the meantime, modern times drew ever closer. The road to Stavig was radically improved by the municipality, and cars traveled day and night. Knut dreamed about having his own car so he could transport potatoes to Molde. His dreams were never fulfilled. Then they both, Lars and Knut, grew old. Knut was seven years younger than Lars and survived him by seventeen years. Knut even wrote a couple of letters to Lars after Lars had passed away. Although he had not heard anything from Lars in a year or two, Knut still hoped he was alive. The letters of Lars Stavig and Knut Stavig, two half-brothers separated by an ocean and decades of time, are a moving story of brotherly love and vast distances and the loneliness and the hopes of the human heart.

NOTES

1. For a history of Norway during this period, *see* T. K. Derry, *A History of Modern Norway, 1814–1972* (Oxford: Clarendon Press, 1973), especially pages 34, 47–49, 137–38.

2. Ibid.

3. Odd S. Lovoll, *Norwegians on the Prairie: Ethnicity and the Development of the Country Town* (Saint Paul: Minnesota Historical Society Press, 2006), pp. 26–27; Theodore C. Blegen, *Norwegian Migration to America, 1825–1860* (Northfield, Minn.: Norwegian–American Historical Association, 1931), p. 162. For more on Hans Nielsen Hauge, *see* Joseph M. Shaw, *Pulpit under the Sky: A Life of Hans Nielsen Hauge* (Minneapolis: Augsburg Publishing House, 1955).

4. Prominent among the Haugean emigrants to the United States was Elling Eielsen, whose lay preaching attracted many followers. Lovoll, *Norwegians on the Prairie*, pp. 115–16; Ingrid Semmingsen, *Norway to America: A History of the Mi-*

gration, trans. Einar Haugen (Minneapolis: University of Minnesota Press, 1978), pp. 65–66.

5. Sverre Mørkhagen, *Farvel Norge: Utvandringen til Amerika, 1825–1975* [Farewell Norway: The immigration to America, 1825–1975] (Oslo, Norway: Gyldendal, 2009), pp. 162–65. This work and two forthcoming volumes are the new standard works on Norwegian emigration to America, and this essay leans heavily on Mørkhagen's work. Another significant historian of emigration is Ingrid Semmingsen, whose major works are *Veien mot vest: Utvandringen fra Norge til Amerika, 1825–1865* (Oslo, Norway: H. Aschehoug & Co., 1941); *Utvandringen mot Vest: Utvandringen fra Norge til Amerika, 1865–1915* (Oslo, Norway: H. Aschehoug & Co., 1950); *Utvandringen og det utflyttede Norge* (Oslo, Norway: H. Aschehoug & Co., 1952); and *En verdensmakt blir til: De forente staters historie* (Oslo: Sverdrup Dahls Forlag, 1946). Semmingsen's book *Drøm og dåd: Utvandringen til Amerika* is available in English as *Norway to America*, cited above.

6. Mørkhagen, *Farvel Norge*, p. 641; Semmingsen, *Norway to America*, pp. 43–47.

7. Mørkhagen, *Farvel Norge*, p. 258. For more on Marcus Thrane, *see* Terje I. Leiren, *Marcus Thrane: A Norwegian Radical in America* (Northfield, Minn.: Norwegian-American Historical Association, 1987).

8. Helge Tveiten, "Sosial uro og utvandring frå Nedenes fogderi," in *Thranerørsla i norske bygder*, ed. Tore Pryser (Oslo, Norway: Samlaget, 1997), pp. 56–68.

9. Mørkhagen, *Farvel Norge*, pp. 641–43; Lovoll, *Norwegians on the Prairie*, p. 6.

10. The Norwegian national poet and politician Bjørnstjerne Bjørnson (1832–1910) visited the United States during the winter of 1880–1881 and returned to Norway with new insight and sympathy for those who had left. Popular songs and popular novels brought emigration up as a theme for conversation in the Norwegian counties. The newspapers printed letters from emigrants, which may have inspired more emigration. Semmingsen, *Norway to America*, pp. 122–23, 165–68.

11. There are also letters to Lars Stavig from other members of his family in Norway and from neighboring immigrants in the United States, among them a letter from a brother of my grandfather, Eilert Knutson Raeknaes, who settled in Donalda, Canada, when the Alberta prairie was opened.

12. Except where otherwise noted, the family information and descriptions of life in rural Norway that appear here and elsewhere throughout this essay are based on a combination of personal experience, family stories, correspondence, and genealogical work conducted over the years.

13. The allodial right still exists, but the period when a close descendant has the right to reclaim a family-owned farm has been reduced to twenty years, and females and males have equal rights. The eldest descendant, male or female, has the right, followed by the next eldest. After all of the children comes the owner's eldest brother or sister and their children, and so on. The system is intended to

keep the farm in the family, even when times are difficult, or when a dishonest owner sells his allodial land. For more on allodial rights generally, *see* "The Allodial Rights Act," www.slf.dep.no/en/property/allodial-rights.

14. Semmingsen, *Norway to America*, p. 109.

15. "Emigranter frå Bergen," Arkivverket.no/digitalarkivet ("Emigrants from Bergen," Digital Archives of Norway).

16. Ingar Sletten Kolloen, *Knut Hamsun: Dreamer and Dissenter*, trans. Deborah Dawkin and Erik Skuggevik (New Haven, Conn.: Yale University Press, 2009), pp. 20–24, 29–30. *See also* Richard Nelson Current, trans. & ed., *Knut Hamsun Remembers America: Essays and Stories, 1885–1949* (Columbia: University of Missouri Press, 2003), pp. 3–8.

17. Semmingsen, *Norway to America*, pp. 129–31; Mørkhagen, *Farvel Norge*, pp. 641–42.

18. "Alfabetiske liste over utvandrarar frå tidlegare Bud, Fræna, og Hustad kommunar etter oppgåve frå Statsarkivet I Bergen for tidsrommet 1874–1930," *Gammalt frå Fræna 2000*, Elnesvågen 2000, pp. 290–354.

19. Mørkhagen, *Farvel Norge*, pp. 62–63; Semmingsen, *Norway to America*, pp. 57, 62.

20. Norway, Central Bureau of Statistics, "Tabell 3.2 Hjemmehørende folkemengde, etter fylke. 1 000," www.ssb.no/a/histstat/tabeller/3-2.html; "Resultaterne af folketællingen i Norge i januar 1866: udgivne af Departementet for det Indre (Norges officielle Statistik, 1868–69) Kristiania: Departementet," p. 291, http://www.ssb.no/a/folketellinger/fob1866.html; Knut Kjeldstadli, *Oslo bys historie bind 4* (Oslo, 1994). *See also* Semmingsen, *Norway to America*, pp. 106–7.

21. In the sixteenth and seventeenth century the forests were cut down and exported for Holland and England, where they became the piles that Amsterdam is built upon and the mast of the English sailing ships that ruled the waves. T. K. Derry, *History of Modern Norway*, p. 1.

22. The account that follows is from Lars Stavig, *Memories of Lars A. Stavig* ([Sisseton, S.Dak.:] By the Author, n.d.), pp. 2–5. *See also* Rasmus Sunde, *Amerikabrev, 1880–1950: Livssoga til to brør frå Romsdal* (America letters, 1880–1950: The life story of two brothers from Romsdal) (Førde, Norway: Selja Forlag, 2009), pp. 47–56.

23. A king's deed of conveyance (*kongeskjøte*) is a transfer of church property in the name of the king, who was the head of the Norwegian church, to the peasants after the Lutheran reformation and also in the nineteenth century. *Norsk historisk leksikon: Kultur og Samfunn ca 1500–1800* [Norwegian Historical Encyclopedia] (Oslo, Norway: Cappelen Academisk Forlag, 1999), p. 210.

24. Sunde, *Amerikabrev*, p. 48.

25. *See Bygdebøk for Fræna*, vol. 2, *Gard og slekt, Elnesvågen 2004*, pp. 155–56. Each *bygedebøk* covers a small area in Norway and lists the farms and owners over many generations. "Bygdebøker," homepages.rootsweb.ancestry.com/~norway

/bygdebok.html. Mathias Stavik is mentioned in the letters, and he himself writes to Lars Stavig. In 1892, Mathias bought a farm some miles from Stavik. He had three cows and was handling the telephone station. For twenty-eight years he also had a store with all kinds of goods, and he asked Lars's son to send him things that he could sell in his own store. Mathias also hoped that he could send his son to America, say the letters.

26. Sunde, *Amerikabrev*, p. 48.

Norwegian Immigration to the United States and the Northern Great Plains

BETTY A. BERGLAND

When thirty-two-year-old Lars Stavig and his wife Maren Hustad with their three children —Andrew, aged seven; Hans, aged four; and Magnus, aged two—arrived in western Minnesota in June of 1876, they participated in the mass migration of Norwegians seeking opportunity in the West.[1] In the century before the major wave of migration, from 1750 to 1850, Norway's population doubled. Such a dramatic increase created harsh conditions for the people, especially in the agricultural areas where more than one-half of all Norwegians found their livelihood. The fact that only one-quarter of the country's land could be cultivated, and much of that was forested, made the problem of population growth all the more severe.[2] The emerging industrial economy of the nineteenth century also threatened the deeply rooted, agrarian way of life, drawing young men and women away from rural areas and toward new jobs in the towns and cities, often a first step toward emigration. These dramatic changes in Norway meant that migration provided a reasonable option for many Norwegians and offered real hope for a better future. The experiences of the Stavig family, as expressed over decades of correspondence, give insight into the lives of countless emigrants who left Norway for opportunities in the new world.

In the nineteenth century, Norwegian society remained highly stratified. The upper class (*kondisjonerte*), represented only 2 percent of the population and consisted of wealthy merchants, large landholders, shipbuilders, sea captains, mine and mill operators, and professionally trained leaders, such as clergy, physicians, and civil servants. The remaining 98 percent was divided almost equally between a middle class, made up of small landowners, craftsmen, and small businessmen, and a lower class, made up of servants, day laborers, and cotters (*husmenn*) who may have owned land but more often worked for others. Norway's population growth created emerging ranks of the landless: children unable to inherit land and small farmers burdened by taxes that led to foreclosures, both factors that served to move the middle classes into the lower classes. In the mid-nineteenth century, most emigrants were middle-class farmers; later, cotters and day laborers dominated the emigrant population.[3]

Norwegian emigrants represented a relatively small segment (814,995) of the vast European migration (about 45 million) to the United States in the century between 1820 and 1920,[4] but Norwegian migration remains significant in two distinctive ways. First, a higher percentage of Norway's citizens migrated than that of any other European nation except Ireland until Italian emigrants replaced Norwegians in that ranking in 1890. Second, more than any other immigrant group, Norwegians sought land and pursued farming and agricultural work. Such was the case as late as 1910 and remained true even into the second generation.[5] In other words, most Norwegians sought out the agrarian way of life that was becoming difficult to achieve in nineteenth-century Norway. Thus, when Lars Stavig filed a land claim in 1883, he represented a long tradition of Norwegians who sought to preserve an agricultural way of life in the new world.

Norwegian emigration to the United States is often viewed as occurring in waves. The first Norwegians to emigrate were fifty-two persons who left Stavanger in western Norway on the sloop *Restauration* on 4 July 1825. Often referred to as the "Sloopers," the passengers and crew pursued migration primarily as religious dissenters—both adherents to Quakerism and followers of Hans Nielsen Hauge, a pietistic lay preacher who challenged the Lutheran state church and gained numerous supporters, especially in the region around Stavanger. The Sloopers hired Cleng Peerson (1782–1865), viewed as the pathfinder for early emigrants, to find

The harbor at Bergen was the point of departure for many emigrants leaving Norway for the United States. The fish market section is shown in this view recorded in the 1870s. (Knud Knudsen photograph, University of Bergen Library, Bergen, Norway)

land and prepare the way; they settled in Kendall Township in upstate New York. This pioneer venture did not directly stimulate later waves of emigration, but the journey is seen as the first chapter in Norwegian migration and provided a contact point in the new world for later waves.[6]

Annual migrations began in 1836 as news of the Kendall settlement and opportunities on the other side of the Atlantic spread through the Norwegian districts. In the next decades—the 1830s, 1840s, and 1850s—a mostly rural and family migration grew, first from mountainous areas in Telemark and the fjord region of western Norway, especially around Sogn, and then from other areas of Norway.[7] By the 1850s, all nineteen Norwegian counties (*fylker*) sent varying numbers of emigrants to America.

The first migration of Norwegians into the Midwest began in 1834 at the Fox River settlement in and around LaSalle County in northeastern Illinois with families from the Kendall settlement and in 1836 and 1837 with immigrants directly from Norway. Following the Black Hawk War and the establishment of Wisconsin Territory in 1836, white settlement expanded westward. The first Norwegian immigrants in Wisconsin Territory, Ole and Ansten Nattestad, arrived in 1837, followed by thousands over the next decades. Settlements grew up in the southern counties of Rock, Lafayette, and Dane and later along the western border of Wisconsin. These immigrants came primarily in family groups, seeking agricultural land to farm. The area's woodlands, punctuated by rivers and open areas, provided immigrants with the resources to build homes, cultivate farms, and create thriving communities. Most prominent were Muskego, Jefferson Prairie, Rock Prairie, and Koshkonong near Madison in Dane County. In the 1840s, Cleng Peerson also served as a pathfinder for a settlement in Texas, but the major pre-Civil War migrations went into the Midwest.[8]

By the 1850s, Norwegian immigrants had moved over the Wisconsin border into northeastern Iowa and southeastern Minnesota. The federal census for 1860, however, identified the highest concentration of midwestern Norwegians in the state of Wisconsin; it claimed 19,758 Norwegian-born residents and 9,799 who had been born in America to Norwegian parents, for a total of 29,557. Minnesota was next, with first- and second-generation Norwegians totaling 11,893 persons. Iowa and Illinois followed with 8,048 and 2,489 first- and second-generation Norwegians, respectively.[9] Clearly, the direction of the new immigrants was northwesterly.

During the period from 1825 to 1865, identified as the founding phase of migration by historian Odd S. Lovoll, 77,873 Norwegians migrated to the United States. More than half of that number (39,350) came in the decade before and during the Civil War (1856 to 1865). The year 1861 marked the height of immigration in that decade, suggesting a growing interest in migration, fueled by newspaper reports and letters sent home from those who had already arrived.[10] These early immigrants and the settlements they founded are important not only because they represent the first communities of Norwegians in the Midwest, but also because they established the first Norwegian institutions—churches, newspapers, schools—and served as the mother colonies for subsequent settlements in the western territories. Often, it was the grown children from these settlements in Wisconsin, Minnesota, and Iowa who sought land and opportunity farther west.

Most Norwegian immigrants, whether they came with the first or subsequent waves, migrated for economic reasons and not for reasons of religious persecution or dissent. Many, however, brought with them a strong religious faith, and establishing a religious community thus became one of the first priorities. During the founding phase of migration, numerous churches emerged in Wisconsin. Most Norwegian immigrants identified with Lutheranism, yet religious dissent and a lay church movement also migrated to the new world. The Lutheran state church in Norway trained and ordained clergy in accordance with doctrinal expectations, but in the early nineteenth century a lay church movement began, led most prominently by Hans Nielsen Hauge. The lay preachers lacked official authority but gained support generally among the laboring classes, many of whom emigrated. Elling Eielsen arrived at the Fox River settlement in Illinois in 1839 and established the first lay congregation in Wisconsin in 1842. In the following year, Claus Clausen organized the first Norwegian American church affiliated with the state church of Norway in the Muskego settlement. In 1844, the first university-trained pastor from Norway, J. W. C. Dietrichson, assumed responsibility in a Norwegian American community. He delivered his first sermon beneath two oak trees in Dane County, Wisconsin, marking the beginning of the Koshkonong Church in one of the important early colonies.[11]

These early developments reveal the importance of establishing churches in the new world. A central concern for communities supporting the Norwegian Lutheran Synod was securing trained clergymen on the frontier, for few Norwegian clergy demonstrated interest. One solution to the problem was the establishment of a Norwegian division at Concordia Theological Seminary in Saint Louis, Missouri, an institution organized by German Lutherans. In the wake of the Civil War and controversies over slavery and doctrinal issues, however, the Norwegian Synod moved its seminary to Madison, Wisconsin, in 1876 and later to Saint Paul, Minnesota.[12]

The founding colonies in Wisconsin established not only the first churches but also other institutions critical for Norwegian immigrant communities, such as newspapers. The weekly *Nordlyset* (*Northern Lights*) was first issued 29 July 1847 from the Muskego settlement near Milwaukee, printed at Even Heg's log cabin by a group of community leaders. It became the first of hundreds of Norwegian American newspapers published across the country. Most immigrant groups established ethnic presses in the United States to provide news of the homeland, the new world, and their communities in the mother tongue; the Norwegian American presses, however, were especially prolific. From 1847 to 2010, more than 280 Norwegian American secular newspapers were published in the United States.[13]

Other institutions important for Norwegian American communities reflect the high value immigrants placed on education, health, and social welfare. Once Norwegian communities were firmly established in the Midwest, the foundation of preparatory schools and post-secondary schools became a priority. Luther College, established in 1861 in Decorah, Iowa, to prepare young men for the seminary, was the first major Norwegian Lutheran institution of higher learning. It later offered other vocational pursuits and opened its doors to both men and women. Most of the Norwegian American educational institutions of higher learning that emerged in the post-Civil War era were clustered in the Midwest and owe their existence to a movement among church leaders to provide young people with an education specifically Christian in spirit.[14] Norwegian immigrants also established hospitals, nursing programs, orphanages, elder care, an Indian mission, and numerous fraternal organizations. These institutions initially served primarily the immigrant populations but later expanded their outreach.

The true mass migration from Norway developed after the conclusion of the Civil War, starting in 1866 and continuing up until the start of World War I in 1914. It was during this period that Lars Stavig and his family arrived in the United States, along with 80 percent of all Norwegians who emigrated. Many single immigrants came seeking opportunities in urban areas during this period; others, like the Stavigs, traveled as families seeking land. Historians refer to the forces that motivate emigrants to leave their homelands as "push factors" and the forces such as land and jobs that draw them elsewhere as "pull factors." The Homestead Act of 1862 served as an important "pull" factor for immigrants in the post-Civil War era. This legislation enabled Americans and immigrants alike, both men and women, the opportunity to claim 160 acres of public land for a small filing fee and gain title by living on the land and improving it over a five-year period.[15] As much of the land in desired regions of Wisconsin was taken, immigrants looked westward to Minnesota and Dakota Territory. Some ventured even further, and by the turn of the twentieth century, migration to the Pacific Northwest had grown. There, farming was supplemented by fishing and the lumber industry, while urban areas, especially Seattle, also held attractions.

Meanwhile, population growth in Norway continued to provide the "push" factor. Norwegian emigration peaked in 1882 as many young, single immigrants left their homeland for opportunities in the industrial centers of Chicago, Minneapolis, Seattle, and Brooklyn, New York, where significant Norwegian settlements developed.[16] Young women with experience in domestic service saw prospects in the United States as more promising than in Norway, while others pursued work in the needle trades or in health care.[17] Young men might seek positions in urban areas as laborers, farm hands, skilled workers, or craftsmen, while some pursued higher education. This pattern is evident with the children of Lars Stavig, who pursued business opportunities in Sisseton, South Dakota, after higher education and eventually built a thriving retail establishment. Second-generation Norwegian immigrants from the midwestern heartland also pursued jobs and opportunities in the urban areas.

While the post-Civil War era offered expanding opportunities in the industrial and urban sectors, for many Norwegian immigrants and their children, the lure of farming persisted, even into the twentieth century.[18] In fact, emigration from Norway to the United States was largely an agricultural migration. Nearly three-quarters of Norwegian immigrants came from rural districts, and in the new world they were the most rural of all immigrant groups.[19] The pre-Civil War Norwegian settlements were essentially rural and agricultural communities; for these immigrants, acquiring land and en-

Pamphlets such as this "official encyclopedia" published by the South Dakota Immigration Bureau encouraged Norwegian immigrants to settle in the state. (South Dakota State Historical Society, Pierre)

gaging in farming not only provided a means of economic survival that drew upon familiar skills but also offered a way of life, thus preserving the culture and agrarian traditions of Norway.[20] Such was also the case for many of those who sought land in the period of industrialization after the Civil War.

By the mid-1870s, immigrants were flooding onto the plains of Kansas, Nebraska, and Dakota Territory, even though earlier generations, including decision-makers in Washington, D.C., had once viewed the Great Plains as the "Great American Desert," an inhospitable wasteland unsuited for white habitation.[21] This region in the nation's center stretches from the Canadian provinces of Alberta, Manitoba, and Saskatchewan to the Rio Grande and from the Missouri River to the Rocky Mountains. Sometimes called the "heartland," it includes North and South Dakota; eastern Montana, Wyoming, and Colorado; most of Nebraska, Kansas, and Oklahoma; eastern New Mexico and most of Texas. Norwegian settlement during the period of mass migration occurred in all of the Great Plains states but most significantly in Dakota Territory, which became North Dakota and South Dakota.

The settlers homesteading on the Northern Great Plains encountered a landscape much different from what they had found in either Europe or the forested areas of Wisconsin, Minnesota, and farther east: few trees, less rainfall, violent storms with hail, high winds, and tornadoes, and seasonal weather with extremes. In the winter, blizzards with severe cold, snowfall, and high winds would form significant drifts; in the summer, hot, dry winds could parch the soil, sometimes forming billowing clouds of dirt.[22] Although the landscape is not entirely flat, the topography and vegetation are less varied than farther east. Two features of the plains proved especially difficult for settlers: the lack of trees made it difficult to build houses, barns, and fences, and the scarcity of water limited the crops that could be grown. Often, the first pioneers to arrive selected their land based on its proximity to flowing water.[23] Wheat, which tolerated the dry conditions, came to dominate agricultural production in the Great Plains. When Lars Stavig wrote home to Norway of his first harvest in Dakota, he wrote of wheat.

Although Dakota Territory had been established in 1861, the eruption of the Civil War, continuing Indian conflicts, and the absence of railroad access delayed extensive settlement until the early 1870s. What drew settlers to Dakota Territory in the 1870s and especially in the 1880s centered on several forces: federal policies, promotional efforts, the demand for agricultural land, and most critically, the railroad. With the passage of the Pacific Railroad Act of 1862 and the completion of the first transcontinental railroad in 1869, the federal government provided land grants to railroads, making them a formidable power in westward expansion. Beginning in the late 1870s, the Chicago & North Western and the Chicago, Milwaukee, & Saint Paul rail lines penetrated southern Dakota Territory, and by 1882 the Northern Pacific Railroad crossed northern Dakota Territory. The railroads themselves promoted farming in the region and encouraged settlement in order to generate revenue to expand their vast transportation systems. Publicity provided by newspapers, land companies, steamship lines, and the territorial immigration commission, combined with the exchange of thousands of letters between Dakota Territory and Norway, all fed the demand for land.[24] During the early 1880s, the population of Dakota Territory soared so that by the end of the decade (1889) both the northern and southern sections had earned statehood.

The immigration of Norwegians and others into the portion of Dakota Territory that became South Dakota occurred in several waves, as geographer Robert C. Ostergren writes, "during three distinct economic boom periods—1868–1873, 1879–1886, and 1902–1915." The earliest period of settlement occurred in the southeastern counties of Union, Clay, and Yankton, which saw the arrival of "Old Americans," or Yankees, who counted roughly half of the population. In addition, however, many Scandinavians, especially Swedes and Norwegians, came in family groups directly from rural districts in their homelands, where they had suffered from poor harvests and food shortages.[25] The second economic boom (1879–1886), during which Lars Stavig claimed his land, reflected a more varied settlement pattern, according to Ostergren. It consisted of "Old Americans" and a more diverse foreign-born population, as well as offspring from established settlements in Wisconsin, Minnesota, and Iowa. Among the latter were many Norwegians who had been brought to those frontiers twenty or thirty years earlier but now sought more opportunity on the Dakota prairies and plains.[26] This area of settlement occurred in the "row counties" of eastern South Dakota, bordering on Minnesota, where Norwegians constituted more than 50 percent of the foreign-born population.[27] Lars Stavig's claim in Day County is in the northeastern corner of the state, one county west of the Minnesota border, but still heavily Norwegian. The third economic boom (1902–1915) and the settlement pattern it generated reflects yet a different pattern: settlers were recruited from the central and southern plains, from older settlements in eastern South Dakota, and from cities in the eastern United States. By 1910, the Norwegian presence in South Dakota stood at 48,721 persons, second only to the Germans as the largest foreign-born population in the state.[28]

Lars Stavig registered his Day County claim seven years after he arrived in the United States, a pattern that was not uncommon. Like many other immigrants, the Stavigs illustrate a pattern of chain migration. Whether traveling singly or in groups, they tended to follow the paths and guidance of family, relatives, or neighbors who had gone before them, much like the links in a chain. The Stavigs' first destination was the farm of Einar Johnson, near Morris, Minnesota, where they remained for three years. This practice of residing first with a relative, neighbor, or friend before establishing one's permanent residence elsewhere (usually farther west) was also common among Norwegian immigrants. Diaries and letters provide numerous examples of this practice over many years of settlement.[29] Three years after arriving in the United States, Lars wrote to his brother Knut of squatting on railroad land, where he also found seasonal work at two dollars a day or four dollars, if he had a horse. Such temporary employment permitted new immigrants to save money to file claims, as Lars did in 1883. He then traveled one hundred miles west with oxen and covered wagon to Roslyn, Dakota Territory, where he claimed his two quarter sections of land. Lars found himself in the company of a significant number of Norwegians. The federal census for 1870 reported 1,284 Norwegians residing in Dakota Territory; by 1880, the number had grown to 22,158.[30]

Lars Stavig, like the others who participated in the land boom of the 1880s, arrived at a good time. A series of wet years, combined with fertile, undepleted soil, gave the new settlers bountiful crops. This boom era diminished by the late 1880s due to drought, over-expansion, declining wheat prices, and, eventually, agricultural depression.[31] During the 1890s, the depression became a national crisis and extended throughout much of the decade. Not until the late 1890s did western migration resume, but by that time the line of settlement, or frontier, had moved into northwestern South Dakota and eastern Montana.[32] This period foreshadowed the other boom-and-bust cycles farmers on the Great Plains would endure over the decades. According to historian Barbara Handy-Marchello, those "who successfully risked buying land, who arrived with a little capital, or who settled early enough to improve and expand their farms before 1900" benefitted from the "Golden Age of Agriculture," a period of good prices and good crops that brought comfort and even wealth to farmers.[33] Lars Stavig was among those fortunate who arrived sufficiently early to buy land, develop his farm, and build a cushion against the harder times that came with the depressed markets of the 1890s and 1920s.

Adjustment to life on the Great Plains went beyond securing a livelihood to sustain oneself and a family while acclimating to a vast landscape with few trees, no mountains, and little water. It also meant making cultural adjustments to the English language, to American ways of doing things, and to the country's ethnic diversity. Settling into communities of others who shared the same culture and language aided the adjustment process; historians call these settlements "ethnic clusters" or "ethnic enclaves." Often, these communities were made up of neighbors and relatives who had emigrated from the same region in the homeland. Together, they built ethnic institutions such as churches, newspapers, schools, fraternal lodges, social organizations, and kinship networks. When individuals of a given ethnicity clustered together in large enough numbers, whether in urban or rural settings, their institutions were more likely to thrive and help to mediate the adjustment process.

IDEAL PHOTO CAR.

WEBSTER, S. D.

O. Fiksdal

Farmers line up to deliver sacks of grain to elevators in the area of Webster, Day County, during one of the "boom" years in eastern Dakota Territory. (Stavig House Museum, Sisseton, S.Dak.)

Immigration historians have debated the pace, degree, contexts, and variables affecting assimilation into American culture. They also debate the degree to which immigrants retain and transplant old-world cultural traditions. Today, most historians agree that assimilation and cultural retention develop concurrently and that subsequent generations Americanize over time. While ethnic clustering and the ethnic institutions they spawn help to sustain immigrant cultures, economic necessity often forces assimilation to American ways. "Polemics aside," writes Robert Ostergren, "it is quite reasonable to describe most of South Dakota's early twentieth century rural immigrant society as socially and culturally *ethnic*, but economically *American*."[34]

The first key adjustment immigrants made was economic-based and was made simply in order to survive. With the exception of the German-Russians, few immigrants had much experience with making a living on the prairie or semiarid plains, which could not be farmed using equipment or methods developed for an essentially woodland environment. Ostergren notes that "most immigrant farmers became Americanized rapidly" as a result of experimenting and drawing upon the ideas of others.[35] Most small farmers in the Dakotas like Lars Stavig produced wheat and, later, other crops such as oats, rye, and barley. Most also raised farm animals such as cows, sheep, and chickens, both for food and for market. Given the intense labor farming required, families survived with the contributions of men, women, and children. In his letters, Stavig frequently comments on the critical assistance of his children, although he mentions less about his wife's work on the farm. Women, however, provided needed income through the sale of butter or eggs, but their contributions went much beyond that.

Despite women's vital roles, their farm work and economic contributions have often been overlooked. Barbara Handy-Marchello explains this omission as due to the "patriarchal family relationships and community structures" of the time, in which "farm women seem to have occupied a position subordinate to their husbands and to other men in the community." In fact, these were systemic cultural practices and beliefs that the settlers brought with them. According to Handy-Marchello, they "were moderated by both custom and law" until "'partnership' might be a better descriptor than 'patriarchy.'" She also argues that the instability of wheat farming—and, one could add, the economic cycles of boom and bust—made women's activities on the farm vital to a family's survival and success and not just a source of "pin money."[36] Although proportionally small, women's income was "steady and substantial enough to meet the basic needs of the family no matter the condition of the crops or agricultural markets."[37] Historian Lori Ann Lahlum likewise finds in the letters and diaries of Norwegian immigrant women themselves that their economic contributions in the form of "milking cows, churning butter, and selling dairy products" were essential.[38] Many Norwegian American women also brought important skills such as needleworking that contributed to the family income or took on nonagricultural jobs, such as cleaning houses and businesses, doing laundry, weaving rugs, knitting socks, working as midwives, or working in hotels. Such income could sustain families for extended periods.[39]

Linked to economic survival was social and cultural adjustment; that is, accommodating oneself to the language and ways of the new land. Ethnic clusters helped to ease the adjustments. In addition, studies show that immigrants—especially in the first and often the second generation—tended to marry within the group, a practice known as endogamy. The institution of marriage, especially endogamous marriage, might therefore aid couples and families in the adjustment process: sharing the same language and cultural values, they could negotiate together the challenges of the new land. Ostergren cites the study of ethnic groups in North Dakota by John C. Hudson, who found that endogamy was the rule for all groups and that Norwegians were second only to German-Russians in their preference for marrying within the ethnic group.[40]

Ethnic communities, institutions, and families all helped to sustain settlers as they adjusted to life in a strange land. Institutions, especially the church, served as a nexus for the immigrants' adjustment process. Churches were spiritual centers and places for the performance of the central rituals of life for most Norwegians: baptisms, confirmations, weddings, and funerals. Sunday services also provided opportunities for social interaction, enabling the exchange of news from the home and offering a time for families to rest from routine labors. Women's contributions to the church in the form of fund-raisers and food preparation for special events also helped communities to survive. More than silent worshipers, women in the Norwegian Lutheran churches actively served in multiple capacities, especially through Ladies Aid. Most often, the sale or auction of textiles or garments could generate significant funds to be used for charity, mission work, retiring church debt, or raising funds for new church buildings. Historian Laurann Gilbertson notes that in 1892, for example, a Ladies Aid in Deuel County, South Dakota, raised and donated seven hundred dollars toward the construction of a new church for the Highland congregation.[41]

The immigrants' process of adaptation can also be seen in the continuity of family farms. Historian Kathleen Neils Conzen, a scholar of rural ethnic communities, explains how cultural values shaped the cycle of family farms in different ways: some parents

Churches served as centers of both spiritual and social activity for immigrants. Pictured here is the Grenville Lutheran Church, which Lars Stavig and his family attended during their years on the homestead in Nutley Township. (Stavig House Museum, Sisseton, S.Dak.)

retained children on the farm longer than others and assisted them in acquiring their own farms in exchange for support from the children in the parents' old age; some parents sought to provide land for all of their children equally during their lifetimes; others sought to transfer their land holdings to a single child; and still others placed minimal value on establishing their children in agriculture. The degree to which these values were shared among members of an ethnic group would affect the endurance of ethnic rural communities, Conzen argues. Specifically, she observes differences between German and Scandinavian cultural values and the implications of those differences for ethnic continuity. Rural, clustered German communities, once established, tended to endure and expand with succeeding generations. By contrast, she writes, "some Scandinavian settlements proved less imperialistic and less enduring, placing greater emphasis on the education of children and the achievement of urban opportunity than on farming as a family tradition."[42] Scandinavian farm families, especially Norwegians, tended to support education for the second and third generations, meaning that the farmstead might not remain in the same family over multiple generations, as generally occurred in Norway. This pattern is evi-

In addition to providing essential services, towns were gathering places where immigrants met their neighbors, both those of the same ethnic group and others. This caravan of new arrivals is traveling up First Avenue East in Sisseton during the 1890s. (Stavig House Museum, Sisseton, S.Dak.)

dent in the Stavig family: Lars supports the higher education of his children and, after twenty-five years of farming, rents out the land and moves to town.

The small town, of course, served critical functions for immigrant farmers like Stavig. They provided a source for vital materials such as lumber and farm equipment, cook stoves and window glass, and items essential for daily life, such as coffee, sugar and flour for baking, and yard goods for sewing clothes. Small towns also served as markets for farmers' commodities, including the eggs, butter, and textiles women produced. Beyond meeting the immigrants' material needs, however, small towns provided opportunities for social interaction, both in the form of information sharing and services such as medical care or mail delivery as well as social gatherings, both ethnic and American, such as Fourth of July celebrations, dances, and other festivities. Culturally, the towns provided churches (Andrew Stavig wrote that Sisseton had four), schools, and newspapers. They also offered business opportunities, as we see with the second-generation Stavig sons. Much has been written on frontier towns and their significance, including the way in which they had a leveling effect on settlers; that is, as settlers struggled to survive, class and status differences became muted. Towns also provided a place where diverse ethnic groups converged.[43]

One of the more vexing adjustments for many immigrant families and communities involved the second generation. The American-born children of immigrants often sought assimilation and identified with the culture of their parents' adopted country. This idea is encapsulated in the so-called Hansen's Law, the proposition that the third generation wishes to know what the second generation sought to forget.[44] In the twentieth century, Americanization was made easier by compulsory school laws and the availability of public-school education. Most immigration historians report similar patterns and the inevitable cultural distance between generations, regardless of ancestral group. Thus, much historical scholarship and many ethnic novels address the generational gap between first- and second-generation immigrants. This issue comes up in the Stavig letters, as Lars repeatedly laments his isolation, especially after moving to town, and finds it difficult to converse in his own language with his family.[45]

The experience of Norwegian immigrants on the Great Plains may have no stronger evocation than that found in Ole E. Rølvaag's *Giants in the Earth*. The story of the fictional Per Hansa and Beret Holm—along with their neighbors on the South Dakota prairie— draws heavily on the oral histories, records, and stories of the first Norwegian Americans who settled eastern South Dakota, including the family of Rølvaag's wife, Jennie Berdahl. In the novel, Rølvaag captures the sense of human possibility on the vast grasslands through the inventive and energetic Per, while he captures the sense of loneliness, dread, and fear in the character of Beret, Per's wife. Neighbors, the other characters, evoke the sense of community that helped to sustain pioneers on the prairies and plains. Rølvaag's deep understanding of the immigrant experience, along with his rich imagination, helped to convey the emotional and spiritual dimensions of that journey. Written in Norwegian and published in English in the United States in 1927, the novel, has long been viewed as a classic.[46] Upon publication, *The Nation* described it as the "fullest, finest, and most powerful novel that has been written about pioneer life in America."[47]

Rølvaag, himself an immigrant from Norway, arrived in South Dakota in 1896 and knew firsthand the struggles and adjustments of migration. He fictionalized his own experiences in the autobiographical novel *The Third Life of Per Smevik*, first published in Norwegian in 1912.[48] In this work, Rølvaag tells the story of Per Smevik through a series of letters Per sends home to Norway describing his life on the Dakota prairies. The last chapter, entitled "Losses and Gains," begins with a letter to his "Dear Grief-stricken Father" written upon receiving the news of his mother's death. More broadly, however, the chapter focuses on the losses and gains of migration. Smevik encapsulates these ideas in a letter to his "Dear Brother Andreas" in Norway, in which he "copies" a Fourth of July speech. "Much have I lost, but much I received (*Stort har jeg mistet, men stort jeg fik*)," begins the fictional orator, who goes on to identify many gains: material blessings, a "practical grasp of things," "personal growth," "great freedom," and the "rich variety of opportunities this land has to offer each individual." Balancing the ledger, the speaker notes the losses: the natural beauty of Norway, identification with the homeland, and "spiritual contact with our own people."[49] He concludes with a summary that evokes a tragic sensibility:

When we severed our ties with our Fatherland, we became not only strangers among strangers, but we were cut off from our own nation and became strangers to our own people. Our pulse no longer throbs in rhythm with the hearts of our own kindred. We have become strangers; strangers to those we left, and strangers to those we came to. . . . Let me repeat: We have become outsiders to the people we left, and we are also outsiders among the people to whom we came. Thus we have ceased to be a harmonious part of a greater whole; we have become something apart, something torn loose, without any organic connections either here in America or over in Norway. . . . In short, we have become rootless.[50]

One cannot help but read this speech, at least in part, as an expression of the tension many immigrants lived with. The "letters" Rølvaag presents in his first novel might offer a meaningful framework for comparison with historical immigrant letters, such as those of Lars Stavig.

The "America letters," or *Amerika-brev*—letters written by immigrants to family members in Norway—provided important links to the homeland. Most of these were intended for families, although many circulated within communities, and some were printed in local newspapers. Theodore C. Blegen argued that this correspondence provided the most reliable information about the new world and so "constitute a composite diary of everyday people at the grass roots of American life."[51] For historians and general readers today, the America letters represent an important historical record of Norwegian American migration, but at the time of their writing they also had profound effects. While Lars Stavig never persuaded his brother Knut to migrate, letters did, in fact, stimulate immigration. Furthermore, they helped to sustain families by maintaining connections, offering comfort and solace, and, sometimes, conveying remittances for taxes, mortgages, and debt relief, as seen in the Stavig letters. Scholars of immigration have written much about the immigrant letters: many social historians have drawn upon them for documentary evidence of daily life, while others, such as literary historian Orm Øverland, have argued that they constitute a folk literature of immigration.[52] However one chooses to interpret them, these letters represent a rich source for understanding immigration, and the epistolary exchanges of the Stavig brothers are an exceptional example of the *Amerika-brev*.

The letters written between half-brothers Lars Stavig and Knut Stavig (and other family members) represent not only an extraordinary correspondence within one family, but also myriad other immigrant letters, lost to us or hidden. The Stavig letters can be seen as both typical and atypical. They are atypical, first, because both sides of the correspondence have been preserved; second, because the correspondence spans fifty years, an exceptional length of time; and third, because the brothers generally remain geographically stable, offering continuity of both time and place. All of these factors allow greater knowledge and insight into this extended family over time and on both sides of the Atlantic Ocean. At the same time, the correspondence conveys themes and patterns evident in many America letters, making them typical and representative. Generally, the America letters served many purposes: reporting news of daily lives, such as progress on the farm or in business, or major events like births, marriages, and illnesses; offering comfort and empathy in life's sorrows and joys as correspondents faced crises and enjoyed successes; providing assistance to family in the old world with prepaid tickets and funds to cover debts; and sustaining connections among intimate family members over time and into subsequent generations.

Lars Stavig's letters reflect the purposes and themes found in numerous immigrant letters, providing rich documentary evidence of life on the Dakota prairies and plains for Norwegian immigrants and their children from the late nineteenth century into the first decades of the twentieth century. Although the collection contains occasional correspondence from Lars's adult children, including his daughters, one could argue that it essentially represents a male point of view. Five themes prevail: the physical and economic struggles to survive; the achievements of the family in the new world, along with satisfaction over the decision to emigrate; news of family and responses to family news from abroad; reports of local, national, or world affairs; and, especially in the last decades of Lars's life, a sense of loneliness and alienation.

Perhaps most prominent in the America letters is the theme of daily life and its struggles. While immigrants did not want to cause worry for family back home, they also sought to convey a picture of conditions in America. In one early letter, the thirty-six year-old Lars told his brother, "I hear . . . that you think it is not going well for me. I must answer you about that. I have none of the world's riches which can be counted in so many thousand dollars [but] I have my Maren and coffee for my house the whole year."[53] Knut may have worried over the fact that five years had passed since Lars left Norway and he remained landless, doing seasonal work for the railroad. Lars explained that he was saving money for his land claim and sought to be upbeat by describing the plentiful work. Two years later, in the fall of 1883, Lars filed for two quarter sections of land in Nutley Township, Day County. Yet, even as a landowner, he wrote of ongoing struggles, periodically mentioning hailstorms and a lack of money to pay taxes or hire help. In another letter, he told of a cyclone that ravaged his farm and destroyed his barn and chicken house. Lars does write about the women in his life and shows candor in expressing his affection for his wife and deep grief over her death, yet Maren's daily life remains quite invisible.

Immigrants also wrote back home about their achievements. In 1887, four years after filing his claim, Lars reflected on his decision to come to America. "We are not gathering gold off from the streets," he wrote. "It is easy to earn money, and it is easy to spend it." Even so, he concluded, "A willing and hard working man can improve himself year by year and eventually become an independent owner of much land."[54] He also responded to Knut's questions about farm production, mentioning milk cows, calves, pigs, sheep, and oxen, and crops such as wheat, rye, and oats. He frequently reported on the harvest, emphasizing the productivity of American farms. The year 1887 brought in eighty-seven bushels of wheat, "more potatoes than we needed for the whole year," and plenty food from the garden.[55] Some years were boom years for farmers, such as the following year, when Lars brought in more than one thousand bushels of wheat and sold it at a good price. On 2 March 1888, he wrote of sending tickets for passage to his wife's parents but cautioned that "no one can expect to become independent for the first five years." On another occasion in the late 1880s, he reported the sale not only of wheat, rye and oats, but also sheep (eight) and oxen (three). Had he stayed in Norway, he told his brother, "I would probably be able to make enough to live on; that would be all." Satisfied that migration had been the right decision, he concluded, "Now I'm the owner of two quarters of land and a group of good houses, horses, and farm machinery that are worth a lot. My land is worth more than I can ever imagine. I cry tears of happiness many times."[56]

Like many immigrants, Lars took pride in his children and wrote of their lives and achievements. On 11 April 1896, he reported that his three oldest sons (Andrew, Hans, and Magnus) had their own land and pursued other interests, as well: Andrew was "buying cows on his own and does business with the stock-market in Chicago," while Magnus taught school and helped out on the home farm in the mornings and evenings. Daughter Louise helped her brother Hans and his wife Pauline, and the youngest three children, Anna, Peter and Edwin, were attending school. Two years later, the three oldest sons were all married and working together in their store in Sisseton, along with their sister Louise. In 1898, at the age of fifty-three, Lars wrote that "my work is mostly in the barn," where he tended twenty-eight cows, sixteen horses, twelve sheep, seven pigs, and one hundred chickens. Perhaps not surprisingly, he also told his brother, "I think I'll quit farming. It is too much for me."[57] The second generation had chosen to pursue business, not farming, and by the third generation, Lars wrote, many of his grandchildren were attending St. Olaf College, studying to be "doctors and professors and lawyers. The women are learning all crafts."[58] In other words, they were being supported in pursuing their education and desired vocations.

Commonly, immigrants also reported on births, marriages, illnesses, and deaths within the circle of family and friends. Lars learned in a letter from Knut about his wife's illness, which would lead to an interruption of correspondence, as well as the death of their mother. Most immigrants never returned home to visit or to live after the initial migration, and word of the loss of parents and siblings they had left behind had to be the most difficult news for immigrants to receive. When Knut lost his wife in Norway in 1901 to kidney tuberculosis, with young children yet in the home, the brothers exchanged tender letters of grief, sorrow, and support, and when Lars learned that his remittance had paid the debt on Knut's farm, he wrote, "It makes my heart feel good."[59] Even Lars's son Andrew contributed to the condolences, and daughter Louise wrote that they would have taken in the smallest child had the distance not been so great. These expressions convey a poignant sense of familial bonds built over years by the exchange of letters.

Many immigrant letters also contained exchanges about local, national, and global events. Lars occasionally reported on local matters, especially the cultural changes he witnessed, noting, for example, the growing prevalence of "sins" such as drinking, dancing, and card playing. Local politics are largely absent from his letters, but Lars referred to divisions in the church that "harmed both body and soul."[60] Son Andrew wrote of the technological advances in the town of Sisseton, such as the advent of electricity and telephones. With the entry of the United States into World War I, Lars described the departures of soldiers and, later, local combat fatalities, while Andrew reported on the Spanish Influenza that left many South Dakota residents dead. During the Great Depression, economic conditions were a topic of correspondence to Norway. Invariably, the emphasis was on the personal hardships the Stavig family and their neighbors experienced, but Lars's son Magnus also reported on broader developments, such as the shocking news of the killing of cattle to control prices.

Like other immigrant letters, Lars Stavig's correspondence also conveyed a sensibility that the new land remained strange. When his wife Maren died following a gallstone operation in 1908, Lars rented out the farm and moved to Sisseton, where he spent the last twenty-five years of his life living in one room rented in the home of a son. It is during this time that loneliness and alienation emerge as striking features in the letters, although intimations appear earlier. In 1904, he wrote, "I'm now a stranger to all things at home in Norway," lamenting that he feels cut off from his homeland, seeing no newspaper articles and receiving only Knut's letters.[61] The sense of alienation is also generational. In 1907, he wrote that his youngest son Edwin had left for college and that "all the children are away. It isn't like Norway."[62] A decade later, he conveyed his isolation to brother Knut: "I don't have much news, as I seldom get out. . . . I can't keep up with the times anymore. . . . Everything is strange and has changed."[63] After another decade, in 1928, he wrote, "It is lonesome for me when I don't understand my own family."[64] Because Lars's descendants conversed in the English language, "everything is lost for me—happiness and sorrow."[65] Other immigrants may have been less candid, but the half-century correspondence between brothers enabled Lars to express his feelings openly.

From the filing of the land claim in 1883 to his move into town in 1908 when he became a widower, Lars had spent twenty-five years with his wife developing and expanding the farm, raising seven children, and supporting their advanced studies and chosen vocations. By most standards, Lars Stavig achieved success in the United States and provided well for his descendants. At the same time, he gave voice to feelings of alienation and loneliness during the last twenty-five years of his life. His experience certainly evokes the work of Ole Rølvaag, who captured the lives and inner worlds of pioneers on the prairie and plains as he explored the gains and losses of immigration in fiction. Lars Stavig, in his America letters to his brother, also evoked the world of pioneering immigrants on the Great Plains, providing historical documentation that represents many immigrants. Perhaps they, too, might be considered part of a Norwegian American folk literature.

NOTES

1. Many English-language sources provide readers with a good overview of Norwegian migration, settlement, and adjustments in the United States. For example, Theodore C. Blegen, *Norwegian Migration to America, 1825–1860* (Northfield, Minn.: Norwegian-American Historical Association, 1931), and *Norwegian Migration to America: The American Transition* (Northfield, Minn.: Norwegian-American Historical Association, 1940); Carlton C. Qualey, *Norwegian Settlement in the United States* (Northfield, Minn.: Norwegian-American Historical Association, 1938); Arlow W. Andersen, *The Norwegian-Americans* (Boston: Twayne Publishers, 1975); Ingrid Semmingsen, *Norway to America: A History of the Migration*, trans. Einar Haugen (Minneapolis: University of Minnesota Press, 1978); Odd S. Lovoll, *The Promise of America: A History of the Norwegian-American People* (Minneapolis: University of Minnesota Press, 1984); Jon Gjerde, *From Peasants to Farmers: The Migration from Balestrand, Norway, to the Upper Middle West* (Cambridge, Eng.: Cambridge University Press, 1985); Odd S. Lovoll, *The Promise Fulfilled: A Portrait of Norwegian Americans Today* (Minneapolis: University of Minnesota Press, 1998).

2. Qualey, *Norwegian Settlement*, pp. 7–12. The steep population growth emerged from two primary forces: the introduction of the potato, which sustained populations through economic crises, and smallpox vaccinations, which began in the early 1800s.

3. Lovoll, *Promise of America*, pp. 8–9; Gjerde, *From Peasants to Farmers*, pp. 6–9; Kathleen Stokker, *Remedies and Rituals: Folk Medicine in Norway and the New Land* (Saint Paul: Minnesota Historical Society Press, 2007), pp. 3–5.

4. *See* Roger Daniels, *Coming to America: A History of Immigration and Ethnicity in American Life*, 2d ed. (New York: Perennial, 2002) for an overview of European migration and the term, *century of migration*. Most migrating Nor-

wegians did go to the United States, although in the twentieth century Canada received Norwegian emigrants also. For a detailed comparative study of Norwegian emigrants to the United States and other regions of the globe, *see* Ingrid Semmingsen, *Veien mot vest*: *utvandringen fra Norge til Amerika*, 2 vols. (Oslo: Aschehoug, 1942, 1950).

5. Gjerde, *From Peasants to Farmers*, pp. 4–5.

6. For an introduction to the Sloopers, and Norwegian migration generally, *see* Lovoll, *Promise of America*, pp. 9–11.

7. Jon Gjerde's study of emigration from the western fjord region of Sogn, *From Peasants to Farmers*, provides a rich and detailed examination of this mid-nineteenth century rural migration and illuminates the contours of Norwegian migration generally.

8. Blegen, *Norwegian Migration to America, 1825–1860*, pp. 61–64, 114–15, 141, 185.

9. Qualey, *Norwegian Settlements*, pp. 218, 222, 227, 231.

10. Lovoll, *Promise of America*, pp. 12–13, 28.

11. For a comprehensive history of the church in Norwegian immigrant communities *see*, for example, E. Clifford Nelson and Eugene L. Fevold, *The Lutheran Church among Norwegian-Americans* (Minneapolis, Minn.: Augsburg Publishing House, 1960); Blegen, *Norwegian Migration to America: The American Transition*, pp. 100–174; E. Clifford Nelson, ed., *The Lutherans in North America* (Philadelphia: Fortress Press, 1980); Lovoll, *Promise of America*, pp. 55–72, 97–114; and L. DeAne Lagerquist, *In America the Men Milk the Cows: Factors of Gender, Ethnicity, and Religion in the Americanization of Norwegian-American Women* (Brooklyn, N.Y.: Carlson Publishing, 1991).

12. Other synods situated seminaries in other locations, but with the merger of major Lutheran Synods in 1917 Luther Theological Seminary in Saint Paul focused on training ministers for the Norwegian Lutheran Church in America. *See* Blegen, *Norwegian Migration to America: The American Transition*, pp. 517–42.

13. In his comprehensive study, *Norwegian Newspapers in America: Connecting Norway and the New Land* (Saint Paul: Minnesota Historical Society Press, 2010), Odd Lovoll persuasively argues how vital these newspapers were to communities throughout the country. (It is interesting to note that when the Dakota War broke out in Minnesota in 1862, there were no Norwegian language newspapers in that state, and Norwegian migrants turned to the newspapers in Wisconsin to read reports of the events in their language.)

14. Lovoll, *Promise of America*, p. 110. The five midwestern colleges with roots in the Norwegian Lutheran church had diverse beginnings and changed location, names, or synods, but they do signify the value Norwegian immigrants placed on education. In addition to Luther College, St. Olaf College in Northfield, Minnesota, was founded in 1874, initially as an academy where several of Stavig's children attended school; Augsburg College in Minneapolis, Minnesota, began as a seminary in 1874; Augustana College in Sioux Falls, South Dakota, began in 1884;

and Concordia College in Moorhead, Minnesota, was established in 1891. For a discussion of the early stages of these colleges, *see* Blegen, *Norwegian Migration to America: The American Transition*, pp. 517–42.

15. Lovoll, *Promise of America*, pp. 18, 82.

16. For studies of the urban areas, *see* Odd Lovoll, *A Century of Urban Life: The Norwegians in Chicago before 1930* (Northfield, Minn.: Norwegian-American Historical Association, 1988); David C. Mauk, *The Colony that Rose From the Sea: Norwegian Maritime Migration and Community in Brooklyn, 1850–1910* (Northfield, Minn.: Norwegian-American Historical Association, 1997).

17. For a discussion of Norwegian immigrant women during this period, *see* David C. Mauk, "Finding Their Way in the City: Norwegian Immigrant Women and Their Daughters in Urban Areas, 1880s–1920s," in *Norwegian American Women: Migration, Communities, and Identities*, ed. Betty A. Bergland and Lori Ann Lahlum (Saint Paul: Minnesota Historical Society Press, 2011), pp. 119–54.

18. For an overview of Norwegian migration and settlement in the Dakotas in the post-Civil War era, *see* Blegen, *Norwegian Migration to America: The American Transition*, pp. 480–516, and Qualey, *Norwegian Settlement*, pp. 130–50 (South Dakota), pp. 151–71 (North Dakota).

19. Odd S. Lovoll, *Norwegians on the Prairie: Ethnicity and the Development of the Country Town* (Saint Paul: Minnesota Historical Society Press, in cooperation with the Norwegian-American Historical Association, 2006), p. 4.

20. The idea that migrating to secure land was motivated both by economic interests of survival and by cultural interests of preserving a way of life is discussed at length by a number of scholars including Ingrid Semmingsen and Theodore Blegen. For a recent discussion, *see* Gjerde, *From Peasants to Farmers*, pp. 1–11.

21. Frederick C. Luebke, "Introduction," in *Ethnicity on the Great Plains*, ed. Frederick C. Luebke (Lincoln: University of Nebraska Press, 1980), p. xv.

22. Stephen S. Birdsall, et al., *Regional Landscapes of the United States and Canada*, 7th ed. (Hoboken, N. J.: John Wiley & Sons, 2009), p. 230. The authors also note that the Great Plains as a region "is substantially an academic invention of the twentieth century." The conceptual framework "is an idea used to frame responses to the widespread economic and environmental problems" that emerged in this region during the Great Depression of the 1930s (p. 232). *See also* David J. Wishart, ed., *Encyclopedia of the Great Plains* (Lincoln: University of Nebraska Press, 2004).

23. Birdsall, et al., *Regional Landscapes*, pp. 234, 239–40. The authors point out that the water issue arose because Americans applied English Common Law in North America, granting the landowner all water rights. They argue, this approach was reasonable in the humid east but not on the Great Plains.

24. Herbert S. Schell, *History of South Dakota*, 4th ed., rev. John E. Miller (Pierre: South Dakota State Historical Society Press, 2004), p. 161; Qualey, *Norwegian Settlements*, p. 134. For a detailed discussion of the effects of conditions on politics in the Dakota Territory, *see* Howard Roberts Lamar, *Dakota Territory*,

1861–1889: A Study of Frontier Politics (New Haven, Conn.: Yale University Press, 1956). For a detailed study of the place of the railroads in the development of the Plains, *see* Claire Strom, *Profiting from the Plains: The Great Northern Railway and Corporate Development of the American West* (Seattle: University of Washington Press, 2003). For a focused study, *see* Carroll L. Engelhardt, *Gateway to the Northern Plains: Railroads and the Birth of Fargo and Moorhead* (Minneapolis: University of Minnesota Press, 2007).

25. Ostergren, "European Settlement and Ethnicity Patterns on the Agricultural Frontiers of South Dakota," *South Dakota History* 13 (Spring/Summer, 1983), 56–57.

26. Ostergren, "European Settlement," pp. 58–59. This pattern of children from one generation moving farther west to a frontier is known as "stepwise" or secondary migration. It also meant that in the ethnic communities, immigrants who came directly from Norway could be neighbors of second-generation immigrants from more easterly colonies who were more familiar with American culture and practices.

27. Ostergren, "European Settlement," p. 66. Ostergren also notes that many of the immigrants in the "row counties" were recruited by the Dakota Territory Bureau of Immigration. Such bureaus, and many states had them, sought immigrants, especially from northwestern Europe, to settle the region. For an example of a recruitment guide, *see* James S. Foster, *Outlines of History of the Territory of Dakota and Emigrants' Guide to the Free Lands of the Northwest* (1870; reprint ed., Freeport, N.Y.: Books for Libraries Press, 1971).

28. Ostergren, "European Settlement," p. 64.

29. *See*, for example, *The Diary of Elisabeth Koren, 1853–1855*, trans. and ed. David T. Nelson (Northfield, Minn.: Norwegian-American Historical Association, 1955); *Frontier Mother: The Letters of Gro Svendsen*, trans. and ed. Pauline Farseth and Theodore C. Blegen (Northfield, Minn.: Norwegian-American Historical Association, 1950). Of course, many other examples exist.

30. Qualey, *Norwegian Settlements*, pp. 236–37.

31. Ibid., p. 134.

32. The settlement of northern Dakota Territory (present-day North Dakota) followed a similar pattern of gradual migration in the 1870s and acceleration in the 1880s. The first Norwegians into the region came to the Red River Valley in 1870, inspired by the writings of Paul Hjelm-Hansen, a journalist whose letters appeared in Norwegian and Norwegian American newspapers, such as *Nordisk Folkeblad* or *Fadrelandet og Emigranten*. As in southern Dakota Territory, the line of settlement gradually moved west in the 1890s into western North Dakota and Montana. The federal census for 1900 identifies 73,744 Norwegians in North Dakota, representing 23 percent of the population, and 4,764 Norwegians in Montana. From 1892 to 1905, Scandinavian immigrants in North Dakota are estimated to have represented nearly half (47 percent) of all immigrants to the state. Qualey, *Norwegian Settlements*, pp. 151–54.

33. Handy-Marchello, *Women of the Northern Plains: Gender and Settlement on the Homestead Frontier, 1870–1930* (Saint Paul: Minnesota Historical Society Press, 2005), p. 5. During the Gilded Age, roughly 1877 to 1901, enormous power resided in the hands of the banks, railroads, and financial interests, leaving farmers and laborers especially vulnerable to these cycles of boom and bust. Thus, many farmers in the Dakotas, especially Norwegians, joined new political organizations to address their economic concerns, most notably the Farmers' Alliance, the Populist party, and the Nonpartisan League. For discussion of these organizations, *see* Lamar, *Dakota Territory.*

34. Ostergren, "European Settlement," p. 79 (author's italics).

35. Ibid., pp. 79–80.

36. Handy-Marchello, *Women of the Northern Plains*, pp. 4–5.

37. Ibid., p. 5. Handy-Marchello identifies four basic points on which historians and social scientists agree about farm women on the plains: 1) women's and men's work was "inextricably linked" even though certain tasks might be labeled male or female; 2) women's contributions to the family income were devalued by most institutional representatives engaged in the rural economy; 3) farm women played important roles in rural communities in everything from churches, education, health care, social welfare, and economic and political activities; and 4) scholarship on farm women depends on listening to and trusting the voices of women (p. 11).

38. Lahlum, "'Everything was changed and looked strange': Norwegian Women in South Dakota," *South Dakota History* 35 (Fall 2005): 200–201.

39. Ibid., pp. 206–8. For a first-person account of women's diverse economic activities, *see* "Herding Cows and Waiting Tables: The Diary of Laura Aleta Iversen Abrahamson," *South Dakota History* 20 (Spring 1990): 17–50.

40. Ostergren, "European Settlement," p. 79.

41. Laurann Gilbertson, "Textile Production in Norwegian America," in *Norwegian American Women*, pp. 157–80, 170. *See also* Lahlum, "'Everything was changed,'" pp. 211–12.

42. Conzen, "Historical Approaches to the Study of Rural Ethnic Communities," in *Ethnicity on the Great Plains*, pp. 9–11.

43. Odd Lovoll's *Norwegians on the Prairie* is an important and comprehensive study of Norwegians and small midwestern towns.

44. "Hansen's Law" is named for Marcus Lee Hansen, the pioneer historian of immigration, sometimes called the "father of immigration history," and author of *The Atlantic Migration, 1607–1860: A History of the Continuing Settlement of the United States* (Cambridge, Mass.: Harvard University Press, 1940).

45. For additional perspectives on Norwegians in the Dakotas, *see* the images and postcards taken by Norwegian photographer, O. S. Leeland and the work of American folk art scholar, Cynthia Rubin, "The Postcards of O. S. Leeland: South Dakota Photographer," *Exposure* 37 (2004): 17, and Cynthia Rubin, "Double Vision: O. S. Leeland's Stereographs," *North Dakota Horizons* 2 (Spring 2011): 14.

46. Ole E. Rølvaag, *Giants in the Earth*, trans. Lincoln Colcord and the author (New York: Harper & Brothers, 1927). This work was first published in two volumes, *I de dage* (Oslo: Aschehoug, 1923, 1924). Much has been published on this novel and on the works of Rølvaag generally. For an overview of Rølvaag criticism, *see* Øyvind T. Gulliksen, *Twofold Identities: Norwegian-American Contributions to Midwestern Literature* (New York: Peter Lang, 2004), especially chapter seven, "Reading Immigrant Literature in Two Countries: Rølvaag Criticism since the 1930s," pp. 185–209. For biographies of Rølvaag, *see*, for example, Paul Rigstad, *Rølvaag: His Life and Art* (Lincoln: University of Nebraska Press, 1972) and Einar Haugen, *Ole Edvart Rølvaag* (Boston: Twayne Publishers, 1983).

47. Quoted on back cover of Perennial Classics, paperback edition, O. E. Rølvaag, *Giants in the Earth* (New York, 1927), n.d. *See also* Lovoll, *Promise of America*, p. 140.

48. Rølvaag, *The Third Life of Per Smevik*, trans. Ella Valborg Tweet and Solveig Zempel (Minneapolis, Minn.: Dillon Press, 1971), was first published as *Amerika-Breve* in 1912 under the name Paal Mørck. For a brief biography of Rølvaag and discussion of the work, *see* the introduction to this volume by Ella Valborg Tweet, pp. vii–xxiv. Here, Tweet notes that Rølvaag used a pseudonym because he found the subject matter of this first novel "so personal" (p. xx).

49. Rølvaag, *Third Life of Per Smevik*, pp. 115–29.

50. Ibid., p. 126. For more on Rølvaag's nonfictional writings on immigration, *see* Ole E. Rølvaag, *Concerning Our Heritage*, trans. Solveig Zempel (Northfield, Minn.: Norwegian-American Historical Association, 1998), first published in 1922 as *Omkring Fædrearven*. The excellent introduction explores both Rølvaag's biography, his views on immigration, and treatments of his writings.

51. Blegen, ed., *Land of Their Choice: The Immigrants Write Home* (Minneapolis: University of Minnesota Press, 1955), p. v. This volume is a compilation of Norwegian immigrant letters; many collections of English-language letters from Norwegian immigrants remain available. Early examples include Farseth and Blegen, *Frontier Mother*, focused on Iowa in the 1870s, and C. A. Clausen, ed., *The Lady with the Pen: Elise Wærenskjold in Texas* (Northfield, Minn.: Norwegian-American Historical Association, 1961). *See*, more recently, Solveig Zempel, trans. and ed., *In Their Own Words: Letters from Norwegian Immigrants* (Minneapolis: University of Minnesota Press, 1991), and forthcoming from the Norwegian-American Historical Association, English translations of the multivolume collection of American letters edited by Orm Øverland.

52. Øverland, "Learning to Read Immigrant Letters: Reflections Toward a Textual Theory," in *Norwegian-American Essays*, ed. Øyvind T. Gulliksen (Oslo: NAHA-Norway and the Norwegian Emigrant Museum, 1996), p. 210.

53. Lars Stavig to Knut Stavig, 21 Nov. 1881, acc. no. H2010-052, State Archives Collection, South Dakota State Historical Society, Pierre.

54. Lars Stavig to Knut Stavig, 11 Mar. 1887, ibid.

55. Ibid.

56. Lars Stavig to Knut Stavig, 7 Apr. 1893, ibid.
57. Lars Stavig to Knut Stavig, 12 Dec. 1898, ibid.
58. Lars Stavig to Knut Stavig, 19 Feb. 1923, ibid.
59. Lars Stavig to Knut Stavig, 22 Jan. 1924, ibid.
60. Lars Stavig to Knut Stavig, 24 Jan. 1913, ibid.
61. Lars Stavig to Knut Stavig, 24 Jan. 1904, ibid.
62. Lars Stavig to Knut Stavig, 25 Jan. 1907, ibid.
63. Lars Stavig to Knut Stavig, 29 Dec. 1919, ibid.
64. Lars Stavig to Knut Stavig, 20 Feb. 1928, ibid.
65. Lars Stavig to Knut Stavig, [n.d.] Dec. 1929, ibid.

Contributors

JANE TORNESS RASMUSSEN graduated from Augustana College in Sioux Falls, South Dakota, and taught English in several public schools and at Sisseton Wahpeton College in Sisseton, South Dakota. She is active in the arts and humanities locally and serves on the South Dakota Arts Council. She and her husband, John Rasmussen, work with the Stavig House Museum and the Nicollet Tower and Interpretive Center in Sisseton and are the parents of three adult children: Sarah, Paul, and Carl.

JOHN S. RASMUSSEN graduated from the University of South Dakota and served as an officer in the United States Army during the Vietnam War era. He has been a community banker in Sisseton, South Dakota, for thirty-nine years and president of the Heritage Museums of Roberts County since 1991. His interest and research in local history, personal interviews, and photographic and anecdotal evidence provide the basis for the documentation of the letters presented here.

EDVARD HOEM is a Norwegian novelist and poet whose works have been translated into nine languages and are well known to readers in his homeland. Among his most notable titles are *The Ferry Crossing* (1974), *Ave Eva* (1987), and *"Once again I greet you": My Parents' Story* (2005). He recently completed a four-volume biography of the Norwegian national poet Björnstjerne Björnson. Hoem lives in Oslo and spends summers in Fræna, where he grew up.

BETTY A. BERGLAND is a professor of history at the University of Wisconsin-River Falls, where she teaches twentieth-century United States history, including immigration history. She received a B.A. from St. Olaf College, an M.S. from the University of Wisconsin-Madison, and a Ph.D. from the University of Minnesota. Her many publications emphasize immigration in American history and culture. She recently co-edited, with Lori Ann Lahlum, *Norwegian American Women: Migration, Communities, and Identities* (2011).

Index